PEOPLE WHO ARGUE ARE SICK

PEOPLE
WHO
ARGUE
ARE SICK

OVERCOMING ANGER AND
HEALING AN ARGUMENTATIVE SPIRIT

DR. DUANE CUTHBERTSON

NEW YORK

PEOPLE WHO ARGUE ARE SICK
Overcoming Anger and Healing an Argumentative Spirit

ISBN 978-1-61448-510-0 paperback
ISBN 978-1-61448-511-7 eBook
Library of Congress Control Number: 2012935389

Morgan James Publishing
The Entrepreneurial Publisher
5 Penn Plaza, 23rd Floor,
New York City, New York 10001
(212) 655-5470 office • (516) 908-4496 fax
www.MorganJamesPublishing.com

Cover Design by:
Rachel Lopez
www.r2cdesign.com

Interior Design by:
Bonnie Bushman
bonnie@caboodlegraphics.com

In an effort to support local communities, raise awareness and funds, Morgan James Publishing donates a percentage of all book sales for the life of each book to Habitat for Humanity Peninsula and Greater Williamsburg.

Get involved today, visit
www.MorganJamesBuilds.com.

Habitat
for Humanity®
Peninsula and
Greater Williamsburg
Building Partner

TABLE OF CONTENTS

INTRODUCTION

THE NEED FOR THIS book is epidemic. Our newspapers daily "scream" with incidents of domestic violence. National and international tensions surround us. These pages will have little relevance for you unless you have ever been in an argument. This book will defend the premise that people who argue are sick. The material has the potential to change your life.

The words from the page of the book "jumped" at me. They stated that, "Each of our lives is a narrative...." Did you catch it? Our lives have a "story line."

From a biblical perspective, this realization is even more profound. Psalms 139:13-16 states that God "...made all the delicate, inner parts of my body and knit them together in my mother's womb." Thank You for making me so wonderfully complex! It is amazing to think about. Your workmanship is marvelous—and how well I know it. You were there while I was being formed in utter seclusion! You saw me before I was born and scheduled each day of my life before I began to breathe. Every day was recorded in your book (The Living

Bible). God created you. It is sobering, but He meant for you to have that nose, those ears, and those feet. God affirmed His standard of beauty through you. You are one-of-a-kind. Struggles have been a part of God's processing of your life, and He has brought you to this very point to reshape you. The hope is that this material will initiate dramatic changes in you. Brace yourself for a miracle.

This is my "story," but your interest in this book indicates that perhaps this is your "story," too. I have a lineage of anger through my father, and I had this reinforced by living three years as a child in inner city Detroit. But I have been fortunate. Outside of the ramifications within my home, I have had limited external consequences.

Porkchop's story is different. I first met Porkchop while teaching at the East Tennessee Penitentiary. His mother had died when he was young. His father, who was seldom home, would leave Porkchop in charge of his three younger brothers, saying, "If your brothers give you any trouble, beat the ___ out of them." And he did. He became angry and aggressive. In time, Porkchop wound up in prison for killing a man in a bar fight. There the other inmates knew not to "mess with" Porkchop. They realized that he had a temper (he killed another man while in prison). To the best of my knowledge, Porkchop is now out of prison, but he paid dearly for his anger with many, many years of incarceration.

I am lucidly aware that it is only the grace and sovereignty of God that differentiates my circumstances from Porkchop's. Perhaps as you read this book you are also incarcerated. Or conversely, you might be a pastor of a large church, who is detached from your wife because of years of arguing. This type of struggle has no boundaries.

Let's affirm Ephesians 1:17-18 as our goal through this book. It states, "That the God of our Lord Jesus Christ, the Father of glory, may give unto you the spirit of wisdom and revelation in the knowledge of Him. The eyes of your understanding being enlightened...." How would you like to have God give you the spirit of wisdom and revelation? How would you like to have the "eyes of your understanding enlightened?" By God's grace, that potential is there. Are you getting excited yet?

After three foundational chapters, we will defend our premise that "people who argue are sick." Then after considering some ramifications of the sickness, we will walk together through the healing process. I don't ask much from you... only that you are willing to become an entirely different person.

CHAPTER ONE

BIBLICAL ANTHROPOLOGY—
Tensions Must Have a Source

It is true that there is "nothing new under the sun." Historically, humankind has always experienced tensions and struggles. The challenge of scientific inquiry has been to define, and categorize them. We will be accomplishing this in our examination of the etiology of an argumentative spirit.

Anthropology is the "study of man." Physiology is the "study of normal functions of livings things or their organs." Psychology became the "study of human behavior and mental functions" and sociology the "study of human society and culture." Do you sense with me the quest of science for understanding and precision? I wonder who initially created these terms, and I wonder how long it took for these studies to assume credibility.

My assumption is simple. There is a missing study. What causes stresses and tensions in our lives? Why can these be manifested differently? Some people have alcohol problems.

2 | PEOPLE WHO ARGUE ARE SICK

Some do not. Some people struggle with drugs. For other individuals drugs are not a factor in their lives. And yes, some people struggle with an argumentative spirit.

Let's call our study Biblical Anthropology. Biblical Anthropology is the "science of diagnosing and assessing the etiology (source) of the tensions in man." The definition itself connotes a source. Tension always says something. For those reading this material who counsel, it is imperative that you are able to identify the source of the struggles in your patients. Let's consider some presuppositions:

(1) <u>Struggles manifest interpretive energy.</u> When we interpret the actions of people who are struggling, we not only interpret the external manifestation (depressed, angry, etc...), but we also interpret the "energy" behind the manifestation. Consider momentarily that awesome passage about the tongue in James 3, verse 10 that relates that "out of the same mouth proceedeth blessing and cursing...." Now, praise the Lord, we have never had "blessings and cursings" both come from our mouths. Right? As the father of five children, and at last count eighteen grandchildren, I have always contended that the best stress takes place on the way to church. We find ourselves saying to our children, "Hurry up, sit down, leave your sister alone...." Then we walk into the sanctuary, and relate, "Hi brother, hi sister..." to our fellow parishioners. I am sure on occasion my children thought, "Who is this man?" Thus, as we consider anger or an argumentative spirit, we must consider the source. The energy is being manifested, but from where? Stay tuned.

(2) <u>Struggles are universal.</u> During my adolescence I had a friend whose mother was deaf. They communicated in sign language. When they argued, their fingers would fly. I used to think that perhaps the world would be better if we all communicated in sign language rather than with our tongues. Environmental experiences evoke emotional reactions. What would you feel if you were in the market when a Palestinian bomb exploded and you witnessed death around you? Conversely, what would you feel if Israeli tanks rolled down your street? Imagine, people like Bin Laden "trained" people to become terrorists. They were trained to hate, to be enraged, to be angry, to destroy, and to kill. We can only conjecture the feelings of the terrorist pilots on September 11, 2001, as the planes were about to hit the World Trade Center. Were they sick? Yes, they were, but let me be presumptuous. If struggles within people are universal then so can be the solution. If this book has credibility, then argumentation potentially can be universally modified. For many, this book will release you from your argumentative spirit. The material is not only for international terrorists; it is for you. What do you feel toward your neighbor, your boss, your extended family? Can those feelings go away?

We are all caught in this "human dilemma." We have a "powerful force within us that is striving to destroy us and to lead us into unrighteousness." Sigmund Freud relates to this as the struggle between the "id" and the "ego." The Bible calls it sin. Whether we approach this material as a "religious believer" or as a skeptic, we all can relate to our capacity to be dishonest, immoral, and disillusioned. Dr. Berkhof, the reformed theologian, defined sin as "essentially a breaking away from God, opposition to God and transgression of the laws of God…." King David, after his sin with Bathsheba, prayed "against thee only have I sinned and done this evil in thy sight. Blot out my transgressions, wash me thoroughly from mine iniquity, and cleanse me from my sins" (Ps. 51:1-3). A study of the Hebrew language relates from this passage that our sin nature has at least three parts. The word "transgression" means that we are in a state of rebellion. The word "iniquity" implies that the bent of our lives is away from God. And the word "sin" connotes that we have all missed the mark. We all fall short of God's standard of holiness and righteousness. We might introspect our own rebelliousness. I believe that the strongest evidence for our "sin nature" is that we know something is wrong and we still decide to do it.

Conversely, we have a "good nature." Genesis 1:26-27 states that man was created in the "image of God." God has placed His imprint within us. We all have a "God-like-ness" quality. This was given to us in part to draw us toward God, our heavenly Father. Words and expressions such as conscience, guilt, and altruism come from this quality. Sociologically, this has led to values, morals, and ethics.

Do these two "parts" of us ever come into conflict? Oh… about all the time. It is the "human dilemma." What do you feel when your children talk back? What do you feel when your wife wants you to go shopping? What do you feel when someone cuts in front of you in the store? Note how the good and the bad natures create tension. When I once asked a dentist, who I was counseling, what he did when people did not pay their bills, he said, "Well, I get up in the middle of the night, and throw a rock through one of their windows." He continued, "But I am fair. If it is a little bill, I take out a small window, and if it is a big bill, I take out the front window."

While teaching at East Tennessee Penitentiary, I spoke to a man who was sitting away from other class members. He stopped me, and explained, "You don't want to talk to me. If you talk to me, the others will not talk to you."

"Why?" I inquired.

He continued, "There is an unwritten law in this prison that if you violate a child, you are ostracized by the population. Kill a policeman and you are a hero. Violate a child and you are ostracized." Even in prison there were "unwritten" laws of perceived goodness.

(3) <u>Struggles are unique.</u> The perceptions and constructs of each individual are shaped differently. It starts before birth. God has placed within the child a particular "bent" or temperament (Ps. 139). Temperament is our behavioral style. It is the how rather than the what or the why. It can be defined as the characteristic tempo, rhythmicity, adaptability, energy expenditure, mood, and focus of attention of the child, independently of the content of any specific behavior. Temperament is not interchangeable. Like any other characteristic of an organism, its features can develop and be significantly impacted by environmental circumstances. Few adults are aware of how the nature-nurture interplay has affected them; they don't stop to think that perhaps their defiance in youth translated into aggressiveness in business or that childhood sensitivity continued into adulthood.

Doctors Alexander Thomas, Stella Chess, and Herbert Birch once studied the temperaments of 141 children from thirty- five families over a period of ten years. They summarized their conclusions in their excellent book, *Temperament and Behavior Disorders in Children* (New York University Press). They recognized that "temperament cannot be the heart and body of general theory," but felt that "we must give as much attention to temperament as environment."

Chess, Birch, and Thomas concluded that a child has genetic predispositions in nine areas: activity, rhythmicity, approach or withdrawal, adaptability, intensity of reaction, threshold of responsiveness, quality of mood, distractibility, and attention span and persistence. One researcher suggested that there could be 4,500 variables as to mood, adaptability, etc... among individuals. Is it not amazing how different we all are?

Chess, Birch, and Thomas identified three different temperaments—the easy child, the slow-to-warm-up child, and the difficult child. In my studies, I propose four categories: (1) the defiant child; (2) the irritable child; (3) the sensitive child; and (4) the compliant child.

Let's briefly categorize each of these: (1) The defiant child acts out his feelings, usually responds negatively to new stimuli, and he is constantly striking out to others. His mood is usually negative, and his reactions are intense. (2) The irritable child is determined to get his own way. He has a strong desire to get what he wants. He generally is a very active person and usually hard to lead. (3) The sensitive child demands much attention and affection. In new situations he usually withdraws at first and adapts slowly. He is slow in accepting new people, and can easily develop feelings of depression and loneliness. (4) The compliant child is generally positive in mood. The intensity of his reactions is generally low or mild. He is rapidly adaptable, and generally evokes pleasant responses in other people. Would you categorize yourself as being defiant, irritable, sensitive, or compliant? (You might refer to my book, *Raising Your Child, Not Your Voice* for further information.)

Many years ago, I was privileged to escort some 300 teenagers on a vacation trip to England. It was such a delight to explore this picturesque and historical country. We all fell in love with our witty and verbose "cockney" guide. One day during a personal discussion of Princess Anne and Prince Charles, he concluded his comments with a pointed, rhetorical question, "Duane, would you have been any different if you were born Prince Charles (next King of England)?" My response might shock you. I retorted, "You know, I think I could have done it; in due respect, I don't believe that Prince Charles is any smarter than I am. He just had different parents. It does make a difference who your parents are." It is conjecture, but would you have been different if you were born Chelsea Clinton or Franklin Graham?

Without question the temperament of a child "interacts" with the environment. In correlating environment to temperament, studies relate: (1) a negative child may be more positive if experiences are gentle and favorable; (2) a very adaptable child may become hardened in a hostile home; and (3) a difficult child can become intolerable with excessive discipline. Conversely, in correlating temperament to environment studies relate: (1) the ease or difficulty in caring for the child can be a factor; (2) the degree of congeniality of the child's temperament can be a factor; and (3) the congruence of parental expectation with the child can be a factor.

Thus, when his environment stresses a child, there will be a variance in each child both in response and effect. Pressure can lead to motivation and performance in one child, or conversely, pressure can lead to frustration and ineptness in another. The "make-up" of the individual becomes the deviation.

On the next page is the Cuthbertson Environmental-Stress Inventory. Score all the factors from one through ten. Place the number (between one and ten) that would be most consistent with your home pattern. Add up the numbers and place the total at the bottom. Check the total with the chart for correlation.

FACTOR	DEFINITION AND SCALE	YOUR SCORE
SECURITY	**Meeting emotional needs of the child**	_____
Much love & affection	1-----5-----10	little love & affection
STRETCHING	Your expectations of the child	_____
Push child little	1-----5-----10	push child much
STRESSES	Pressures on child outside home	_____
Little social pressure	1-----5-----10	much social pressure
SHUFFLING	Mobility, how much moving	_____
Moved little	1-----5-----10	moved much
STRUGGLES	Conflict between parents	_____
Little home tension	1-----5-----10	much home tension
SHAPING	Consistency of your lifestyle	_____
Consistent example	1-----5-----10	inconsistent example

CHART CORRELATION:

44-60	Exposed to unreasonable stress
30-43	Above average stress
18-29	Average stress level
0 -17	Perhaps inadequate stress

This is congruous with an argumentative spirit. Let's explore a couple examples. How would excessive "moving" effect a defiant child compared to a compliant child? How would "poor modeling" by the parents impact a sensitive child in contrast to an irritable child? Now, before we leave this discussion, I would hope that all of you have determined both your temperament and your various environmental effects. Without question, each of us brings something different to our discussion on argumentation.

(4) <u>Struggles connote the potential for perfection and wholeness.</u> I have a cartoon of two ministers commenting on a new signboard in front of one of the churches. Across the signboard is the title for the next Sunday sermon "Thou shalt not covet thy neighbor's goods." The one minister asks, "How do you like it (the new signboard)?" The other minister comments, "Very nice..." Then after some reflection he continues, "But I wish we had a signboard like that at our church." I love it. Our society thrives on a context of excellence. We pay professional athletes millions... (that's millions) of dollars... to play adolescents' games. We give A's, B's, and F's for grades in our schools. Don't you love the bumper sticker, "My son/daughter is an honor student at such and such..."

David Myers, in his book *Social Psychology*, defines a self-serving bias as "the tendency to perceive oneself favorably." Perception is everything. There is reality as it is and reality as we perceive it. When two individuals perceive reality differently, there is the potential for tension. Psychologically, this is called cognitive dissonance, which Myers defines as "feelings of tension that arise when one is simultaneously aware of two inconsistent cognitions." Said more simply, my spouse would be better if he/ she were more like me. I submit that in the best of marriages the pretext is that we will change our spouse. Consciously and subconsciously, for some, this leads to an "oneness" in the relationship. For others they "argue" the same issues over and over and over…. The "oneness" never occurs. I know it's hard to believe, but there are people who argue more than once over the same issue.

Any tension… any attempt through argumentation to change another's opinion connotes an ideal. Rationally and intuitively we believe that we are correct. Why?

Let's explore three arguments for this sense of perfection:

<u>A Biblical Defense:</u> Matthew 5:48 states, "Be ye perfect as your Father in Heaven is perfect." The Greek word for perfect connotes "being a full age, mature, complete." The same God, who saw me in my mother's womb before I was born (Ps. 139), is the same God who "called" me before the "foundations of the world" (1 Tim. 1:9). It is the same God who from the outset of my salvation and through my life sees me "whole and complete."

Ephesians 4:12 sets forth a three-fold purpose of the Church: (1) the work of the ministry; (2) the edifying of

the body (the Church); and (3) the "perfecting" of the saints. It is through the Church that I have the potential of becoming "fully equipped" to become the person that God desires to develop. Generally, the church could do better in understanding and developing the "perfect" (complete) saint. In fairness to the church, perhaps the leadership and resources are not available. This concept in practice would involve isolating and developing each person within the church; helping them to recognize their spiritual gifts, putting them to work within the body, and helping them to be equipped.

There is an antithesis. Many years ago while involved in Christian radio, I created and produced a daily interview program. In one of the interviews a guest was expounding on a verse from the Bible. John 10:10 states, "The thief comes to steal, kill, and destroy… but I come that ye might have life and have it more abundantly." The lady commenting on this passage expounded that she believed "The devil here is giving to us his game plan." She continued, "The first thing that he does is steal our joy, then he kills our spirit (the depression and frustration), and finally, he destroys our soul and body." I was aware that this was conjecture, but the profoundness hit me immediately. Most of us have been unhappy at some point in our lives. I retorted, "There are two ramifications from your comments: (1) I am never going to be unhappy another day of my life; and (2) Everything that is negative comes from Hell itself." So the boundaries are set. God is striving to move us toward "completeness" and the devil is striving to "destroy" us.

I trust that you understand that this "completeness" is not "sinless perfection." It connotes the reaching of our full potential. I believe it to be synonymous with what theorists such as Abraham Maslow and Carl Jung discuss as "self-actualization" and "individuation." It is interesting that both the theological and psychological communities are striving to understand this "complete" person.

A Pragmatic Defense: As I have already implied, this is a sociological defense. I call it intimidation by perfection. As I previously stated, society has created a context of excellence. As of this writing, a star athlete for the Detroit Tigers baseball team is signing a contract for some seven million dollars a year. I contend that no athlete is worth $7,000,000. The president of the United States makes some $400,000 a year. One hits a baseball. The other has the responsibilities of directing a nation. How did we create a society in which an athlete makes overwhelmingly more money than the president? The "perfection" is intuitive. Are we not all experts on raising the neighbor's kids? And do we not have opinions about everything? This context of "intuitive perfection" has permeated the socialization process. We consider some people more "religious" than others. We consider some people better "looking" than others. This etiology of "perfection" must come from within man himself. In the Bible, as early as Genesis, chapter four, Cain was "jealous" of his brother Abel. He became angry and killed him.

The Philosophical Defense: My college philosophy professor had just related that Socrates believed "that everything was relative, but if everything was relative then there had to be an absolute." He continued as he wandered around class and touched a desk, "this is not really a chair, it is a symbol of a chair, but the fact that we call it a chair means somewhere, at least conceptually, there is an ideal chair...." The class then enjoyed the process of creating that ideal chair with its soft cushions, built-in refrigerator, etc.

But I was not ready for his next scenario. He continued his walk about the classroom and he began putting his hands on the shoulders of various students. He commented, "This is not really a Davis. This is a symbol of a Davis, but somewhere out there is an ideal Davis. This is not really a Cuthbertson. This is a symbol of a Cuthbertson, but somewhere out there is an ideal Cuthbertson." Put in your own name in the blanks. This is not really a _____. This is a symbol of a _____. Somewhere out there is an ideal _____. Theologically, sociologically, and philosophically an "ideal" us is attainable. The way that we respond to our struggles communicates whether we are advancing or declining. Many, however, have neither the perception nor insight to understand. So we argue and argue and argue again. Before we can understand the dysfunctional, we must understand the functional. If we know what has broken down, we can better understand how to fix it. So hold on tight, I repeat, "People who argue are sick."

CHAPTER TWO

PSYCHOPHYSICAL UNITY—
Understanding Maladaptive Instincts

O ur quest is to find the source of an argumentative spirit. It was my delight to teach "Abnormal Psychology" at William Tyndale College in Michigan. I taught my students that their intervention with others will be limited if you can't diagnose the individual's problem. This chapter will lay the foundation in "diagnosing" the "structure of man."

Maybe I am presumptuous. Forgive me. I am aware that our church fathers have debated this issue since the second century. Is man dichotomous (two parts: spiritual and physical) or is he trichotomous (three parts: spirit, soul, and body)? David Myers and Malcolm Jeeves in their book *Psychology Through the Eyes of Faith* defend what they call "a psychophysical unity." Using philosophy and support from the Old and New Testaments, they demonstrate that biblical passages emphasize wholeness. "The details of Hebrew psychology differ from the details of contemporary science, but one fundamental point on which they both agree; mind and emotions are inextricably linked with the body. The people of the Old Testament thought with their hearts, felt with their bowels, and their flesh longed for God. Of the body organs the heart was the most important. In the 851 Old Testament uses of heart, it continually denotes the whole personality...." Of course, we exist as a whole person. But does that not imply that the whole will be influenced by its parts? Now we must ask if there is enough biblical distinction to divide the spirit and the soul. I contend that the strongest argument for this is that in Scripture, and I am aware that this is not all- inclusive; we have three different words used for the structure of man. We also have Scriptures that refer to three "differential" parts within this same context. Church Father Origen strongly accepted and defended this trichotomous conclusion as being consistent with Scripture. "Origen even took the words soma (body), psyche (soul) and pneuma (spirit) as clues to the proper method of interpreting all Scripture." I believe that the church is indebted to him for his insight. I will utilize this structure throughout this material.

Genesis 2:7 relates the creation of man: "And the Lord God formed man of the dust of the ground, and breathed into his nostrils the breath of life; and man became a living soul." Note that Adam was made from the dust of the earth (body), and God breathed into him the breath of life (spirit), and he became a living soul (soul). Hebrews 4:12 comments on the power of the Word of God, how it can "pierce asunder... dividing soul and spirit, and of the joints and marrow (body)…." Notice in both of these passages is the assumption that man has three parts.

The strongest biblical passage in defense of man being trichotomous is found in 1 Thessalonians 5:23, "And the very God of peace sanctify you wholly, and I pray God that your whole spirit, soul, and body be preserved blameless unto the coming of our Lord Jesus Christ." Are you ready to get excited? Notice that the concept of "perfection and completeness" is not only emphasized in this tri-part "structural analysis," but God was so determined that we didn't miss the point, that He emphasized the concept of wholeness twice in the passage. "Sanctify you <u>wholly</u> (completely)… that your <u>whole</u> spirit, soul, and body…."

In the *Evangelical Dictionary of Theology,* W.E. Ward states that "the present theological and psychological emphasis is based almost altogether upon the fundamental wholeness or unity of man's being and against all philosophical attempts to divide him." Our evangelical seminaries teach hermeneutically to exegete biblically from the smallest to the largest, and the Scriptures state that every "jot and tittle" (smallest parts of the Hebrew language in Holy Writ) is inspired. Yet, we still have avoided the challenge of applying these same principles to psychology. Gestalt psychology views man as a whole. The Reductionist starts with the smallest parts and builds to the whole. Philosophically, our approach in this material will be reductionism. What are those parts that affect my argumentative nature?

We have established the premise that God wants us to be whole and complete. Does that not pre-suppose that the "wholeness" must have parts? And for the sake of argument, if the "wholeness" has the potential for completeness, can there be completeness in each of the parts? (Oh, are you getting excited yet?) And psychologically when something "breaks down," what part is breaking down? What then is the origin of an argumentative spirit? How is it fed?

Let's establish some presumptions before we divulge the proposed structure of man.

(1) <u>Interpretative energy can be defined.</u> If I cut myself, I bleed. If I choose to run my car into a tree, there will be devastating results. Many believe that the basic premise of psychology is cause/effect. For every effect, there must be a precipitating cause. All behavior is intrinsically motivated. Why is he drinking alcohol excessively? Why is he taking drugs? Why did his wife choose to become unfaithful? Why do I argue so easily? Our society has a tendency to look at the effect rather than the cause. A number of years ago, there was a television campaign to encourage young people to "just say no" to drugs. Obviously most of us support efforts to stop this repugnant, self- destructive abuse. But the situation is much more complex than just saying no. We have suggested that all "interpretive energy" must have a source, whether it be depression, lust, guilt, and/ or, yes, an argumentative spirit. Once we determine the source, we must begin the process of defining ("breaking it down") and understanding it.

(2) <u>It takes little for individuals to become inoperable.</u> I would like to draw upon the analogy of an automobile. My car can be a "junk car" or a new Cadillac.

If the battery is dead, it will not function. It takes little for the car to become inoperable. When people struggle, it takes little for them to become inoperable.

People say, "So I smoke three packs of cigarettes a day. So I have a drink or two between work and home. So I am having a little affair with the secretary. So I argue with my wife and occasionally hit her." Notice that regardless of the dysfunction, the problem becomes the "focus" point. It can become both obsessive and compulsive. There is both a driving and controlling factor. In addictive disorders, an individual can become preoccupied with the problem. I am not picking on cigarette smokers, but I recall while in graduate school being nudged by a fellow student, who couldn't wait until the class was over so they could have a smoke. I once did a seminar at a little country church. After the Sunday school hour, the majority of the men left the building. I commented to the pastor, "I hope it's not me." He laughed and said, "Come to the door." I looked out and half the men of the church were having a smoke between Sunday school and Church. I wonder where in my talk some of them became obsessed to have a smoke.

(3) <u>God created humans with parts.</u> The Scriptures refer to them as members. As this particular word is used within the Bible, it primarily means "parts of the body." Some have established the argument that the word is physiological not psychological. Passages such as 1 Corinthians 12:12 state, "...the body is one and hath many members...." The verse is forming an analogy of gifts within the Church to different parts of the human body.

The passage continues that "the eye cannot say to the hand that I have no need of thee…" (1 Cor. 12:16). However, there are other verses in which the same Greek word is used with strong psychological ramifications. Romans 6:19 challenges us not to yield our "members" to "become servants to uncleanness and to iniquity…" but to "yield our members servants to righteousness and holiness…." It's time to get excited!! Notice first, that obviously the context of "members" here is more than physiology, but secondly, notice that the results desired, yes demanded by the Lord, are righteousness and holiness. Holiness is the desire to emulate God's character and righteousness is the desire to emulate God's standard. God desires to get some semblance of holiness and righteousness from us. James 4:1 reminds us that wars and fighting come from "lusting and warring within our members…." The last time I checked, my arms and legs were not bickering. But there have been times in my life when I have argued and have gotten angry. The energy had to come from somewhere.

(4) <u>Our members interact and are interdependent.</u> None of these parts stand-alone. I have the privilege of teaching a course entitled "Marriage and Family" at the college. One of things that we discuss is gender differences. For some reason these, eighteen to twenty-two-year-olds are intrigued with the opposite sex. Strange, isn't it? But I love to ask, "What attracts you to the opposite sex? Is it instinct (mating)? Is it sensual (sight, smell, etc…)? Is it emotional (love)? Or is it drive oriented (sex)?" They are such a great group.

And to continue the illustration, each of these parts is involved in dating. Each can stand alone, but usually all "intuitively interact" without conscious effort on our part.

Let's relate this to an argumentative spirit. Proverbs 16:32 states, "He that is slow to anger is better than the mighty; and he that ruleth his spirit than he that taketh a city." Note the correlation between emotions ("slow to anger"), will ("ruleth"), and spirit ("his spirit"). Here are three "parts" of personality interacting to control anger and an argumentative spirit. We are on the verge of our first insight into "healing" anger. What biblical principles are pertinent to rebuilding the emotions, the will, and the spirit? The challenge for the biblical counselor is to "restructure" the individual in these areas.

(5) There is perfection (completeness) within each of the parts. Hebrews 12:23 relates that the "spirit of the just man" may be "made perfect." How does a functional (or perfect) spirit differ from a dysfunctional one? If there is a pathological problem within an individual, how does that affect the human spirit? Can problems of the human spirit be diagnosed as part of the problem? How does all of this affect anger? We will eventually address these questions.

Let's consider another point. Hebrews 9:9, in discussing sacrifices and gifts, states, "they could not make him that did the service perfect, as pertaining to the conscience." Is it possible to have a perfect conscience? Now be careful… that thought could really be stimulating. How would this relate to guilt and peace?

It would seem that the potential for "completeness" is within all of us.

(6) <u>There is perfection within the whole.</u> Can you imagine victory over your argumentative spirit? Can you imagine a perfect spirit, a perfect conscience…? Hebrews 13:21 says that God desires to "make you perfect in every good work to do His will, working in you that which is well pleasing in His sight, through Jesus Christ; to whom be glory for ever and ever." God wants to "make us perfect in every good work to do His will…." There is a constant refining process within us. Our lack of understanding and discernment fuel the devil's workings, and through his "principalities and powers" he continues to wound saints and attempts to keep the Church inordinate and ineffective. We want to change the emphasis from the wound to the healing. Even as you are reading through this material, picture yourself healed. Envision yourself a different person, diffused from anger and an argumentative spirit.

God works through a "purging" process. John 15:2 expounds that principle: "Every branch in me that beareth not fruit he taketh away; and every branch that beareth fruit, he purgeth it, that it may bring forth more fruit." We have some trees and shrubs on our property. Recently, I had to "purge" some limbs attacked by insects. They had eaten the leaves. I am amazed how something blossoms after it has been purged. As you allow God to prune, be ready not only for some changes, but perhaps also be ready for some pain.

(7) <u>There has to be a structure.</u> As we have stated, whether as individuals or as counselors, it is imperative that we have understanding of the structure of man. How did God create us? Do we have parts? How are these parts inter-related? Is there an inter-dependence? When their parts become "maladaptive," what are the consequences?

Here is how I envision the structure of man.

(8) <u>The Parts can be defined.</u> Let's review. We all have tensions that manifest energy. This energy must have a source. Thus, there must be a structure within us. We have parts and the potential for perfection, or completeness, within these parts. If there is the potential for perfection within the parts, then there must be the potential for completeness within the whole. These parts can be defined:

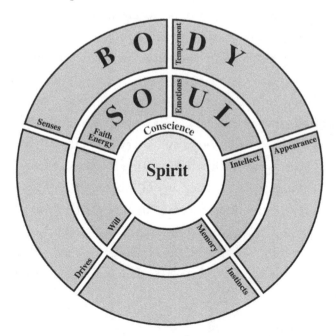

Spirit: is the furnace, the essence of life within man
Soul: is the interpretative part of our personality
Conscience: is God's imprint, our potential for goodness Emotions: are our feelings
Memory: is the storehouse of all our experiences Faith Energy: is the vacuum, or void, of personality Intellect: is the potential for "reflective" thought Will: is the determiner
Body: is the frame
Temperament: is the genetic predisposition
Instincts: are our distinctives Senses: are the doors and windows Appearance: is our image
Drives: are our urges

We will eventually discuss how these interact in expressing argumentation.

(1) Finally, parts within this structure can be "adaptive" or "maladaptive." I am indebted to William Kirwan from his book, *Biblical Concepts of Christian Counseling*. He related:

"When Adam fell, genuine needs were born. The need to belong, the need for self-esteem, and the need for control are now the most prominent driving forces of personality. Do we meet our needs in the positive ways that God has designed thus producing happiness and fulfillment. Or do we try to meet our needs in our own way, which ultimately leads to self destruction?

We would like to think that we meet out needs God's ways. Mavis (previous author quoted by author) notes two inner forces which incline us to wrongdoing as we attempt to meet our needs: first, there are the natural and inborn tendencies, which the theologians have termed original or innate sin. Secondly, there are REPRESSED COMPLEXES AND MALADAPTIVE IMPULSES, which have been acquired in life experiences. Maladaptive impulses are qualitatively different from natural (original) sin. We all have legitimate needs and legitimate impulses to meet these needs. We also have a tendency toward sinful ways. Maladaptive impulses seek the normal ends of life (needs)... wrongly."

He continues by identifying these "infirmities" within us.

"The sincere person on the Christian quest becomes confused and disillusioned when he/she fails to recognize that the Holy Spirit does not cleanse away, like a great divine psychiatrist, all the emotional complexes, defense mechanism, anxieties, and other ineffective psychological process when He fills the human heart with His sanctifying presence. Paul recognized that many of the psychic processes remain in the heart after the filling of the Spirit. After describing personal freedom in the law of sin and death in Romans 8, Paul says, 'Likewise the Spirit also helpeth our infirmities (Romans

8:26).' The Holy Spirit employs a different kind of divine therapy in resolving the acquired tendencies to wrongdoing. He does not remove all of them by an act of cleansing, but rather He helps believers to gain insight into their maladjustments and to resolve them by His strengthening process."

I've got news for you. All of us to some extent are "maladaptive." The emphasis of this material is on anger and an argumentative spirit, but certainly there can be many ways that these "maladaptive instincts" might express themselves. My heritage was one of anger. I had a strong-willed father, and the end result was that I developed "maladaptive instincts" of strong will and anger. I became an argumentative person. Note that this is an "instinct." I began a process of building defenses and walls to survive. We normally don't consciously articulate instincts. Is it not true that married people instinctively want "processes" such as companionship, encouragement, and security?. We can take some very "good things" for granted. But if we intuitively sense unmet needs in our marriage we might become angry and argumentative. It some cases we cannot articulate the problem, but we know that something is missing.

I factiously say to my students, "Counseling is easy. You set before them a biblical context of perfection. You identify the maladaptive instincts, and then you help them to rebuild those maladaptive areas."

The reason that it is not simple is that each individual is different. Some have negatively reinforced "wrong" principles consistently for years. I remember a wonderful rebuke by a dear lady after a conference. I had stated that "practice makes perfect." She commented, "In due respect Dr. Cuthbertson, practice does not make perfect, practicing perfection makes perfect." Her thought was profound. I could graphically illustrate this through my golf game. I have maintained incompetence there for years, but I have never sought help. I have never learned to play the game correctly.

Self-realization is the first step of change. Are you adaptive or maladaptive? The following chart is an attempt to aid you in evaluating yourself. My challenge is for you to be honest, reflective, and accurate.

Adaptive/Maladaptive Behavior

This chart was created to evaluate adaptive/maladaptive behavior. Each statement is worth ten points. When you are finished, add up your score. Grade yourself in each area 1-10, with ten being the highest. Grading scale: 90-100= A, 80-89= B, 70-79= C, 60-69= D, Below 60= F.

(1) Am I more optimistic than pessimistic in my outlook on life? Do others Perceive me to be cheerful and encouraging?
(MY SPIRIT)   _____

(2) Do others perceive me to be a "sweet" person? Do I express a minimal amount of bitterness and cynicism?
(MY SOUL)   _____

(3) Do I have an inner peace and generally feel comfortable with my relationship with God and with others? Do I have a minimal amount of guilt?
(MY CONSCIENCE)   _____

(4) Do others perceive me as a loving and patient person? Do I have a minimal amount of anger and fear in my life?
(MY EMOTIONS)   _____

(5) Do I live in the present? Am I excited about what is presently happening in my life, or is there a tendency to be pre-occupied with experiences from the past?
(MY MEMORY)   _____

(6) Do I have an active and personal faith that is lived and practiced, or am I pre-occupied with "addictive" behavioral tendencies such as cigarettes, alcohol, gambling, etc.?
(MY FAITH ENERGY)   _____

(7) Do I respond well to correction? Would others not perceive me to be a strong-willed person
(MY WILL)   _____

(8) Do I have a self-acceptance of my body? Do I believe that God did not make mistakes when He made me?
(MY APPEARANCE)   _____

(9) Do I keep my body under subjection? Do I have will power when it comes to eating or sexual struggles?
(MY BODY)   _____

(10) Do I understand my own temperament as I respond to pressures, stresses, and struggles?
(MY TEMPERAMENT)   _____

MY SCORE IS _____MY GRADE IS _____

CHAPTER THREE

SPIRIT-SOUL COMPLEXITY

Our quest is to locate the source of anger and argumentation. We have affirmed the concept of Biblical Anthropology, which we defined as the science of diagnosing and assessing the etiology (source) of the tensions in man. We have suggested that we are composed of many parts, and each of these manifest energy. This energy can take on a dimension that is either adaptive or maladaptive. Maladaptive impulses seek to meet the normal needs of life wrongly. Obviously, an argumentative spirit would be a maladaptive impulse. This chapter is our last preliminary chapter before we specifically defend how "people who argue are sick." A better understanding of our "spirit" and "soul" is imperative in this quest.

I first met her in a "safe house." She was hiding from her husband who was out on bond. She had "caught" him in an affair. He was apologetic, begged for forgiveness, and promised her that he would never do it again. She took him back, and she thought that they were reconciled. Some three weeks later he took her to a nice restaurant in Ann Arbor, Michigan. She was to wear her finest clothes. They seemingly had an enjoyable meal, and they were on their way home. Suddenly, he pulled the car onto a back road. To quote her exactly, as she related it to me, "Dr. Cuthbertson, I thought that I was going to be romanced." But, in fact, her husband looked at her with rage pouring from his eyes and said that he was going to kill her. He began to pound her across the face with his fists. She was able to get the car door open. He ran around the car, tackled her, and as she was in absolute hysteria, he held her down with his knees on her arms and proceeded to hit her "back and forth" across the face. In his perverted mind, his intent was to knock her out, place her behind the steering wheel, and push the car over a hill that dropped into a river. Another car had been stashed away for him to make his escape. His plans, however, went awry. When he pushed the car toward the crest of the hill, a small bush stopped the car. At about this same time, another car drove up upon the scene and he had to leave.

Next, she was in a coma at the University of Michigan hospital. The husband was by her side, well aware that if she came out of this coma, he was "fried." A suspicious sister stayed with her continually. In one of the few moments when he was out of the room, she hysterically came out of the coma. He was arrested, and he was presently out on bond (if you can believe that). She was placed in a "safe house." It was through the sister that I was drawn into this.

Her story was devastating. As she shared the details with me, she cried incessantly. She was frightened: she was depressed. She was a broken lady. I will never forget her final comment that evening. In sobbing outcries, she pleaded, "You see, it is not so much what he did to my body, it is what he did to my spirit."

She was correct. Proverbs 15:4 states, "A wholesome tongue is a tree of life, but perverseness therein crushes the spirit." Her spirit had been crushed. As clinicians we will meet patients who have had experiences so traumatic that their spirits are wounded, or crushed, or afflicted.

Now, before we continue, consider with me what this woman felt when this ordeal was over. Do you suppose there was any anger within her? And what could possibly motivate a man to manifest such rage? (He did eventually go to prison.) Now reflect for a moment. Perhaps your life has not been quite so dramatic, but "your narrative life" has had many diverse experiences. What have been the effects upon your spirit, soul, and body?

In this chapter, I will develop biblical principles of the human spirit and soul. First, let's consider some principles of the human spirit.

(1) <u>The human spirit is the essence of life within us.</u> The human spirit is the furnace. In Genesis 2:7 the spirit is defined as the "breath of life," breathed into man by God. When we die, our spirit is released. Note that when Jesus, when He died, gave up His spirit to the Father (Luke 21:46). James 2:26 relates that the "body without the spirit is dead...." We are alive because we have this "furnace," this energy source within us. We are not empowered by the local power company. There are no cords running from us into the wall.

We are an entity within ourselves. Are you getting excited yet? Proverbs 20:27 (NASB) relates that "the spirit of man is the lamp of the Lord, searching all the innermost parts of his being." Words like "candle, lamp, and light," found within Scripture, often relate to this dimension of personality. Vine's *Expository Dictionary of Biblical Words* defines spirit as "the life principle, bestowed upon man by God." Frank Minirith, in his book *Christian Psychiatry,* explains the spirit as "being the supernatural part of man given by God at birth." The definition I like best, however, comes from Frank Deiltsch in his book *A System of Biblical Psychology.* He states, "The spirit which was breathed into man was indeed, the condition of life to his body." The words "condition of life" intrigue me. You see the body of a person, but you perceive a "persona," a personality. In reality, your impression of the person comes basically from his or her spirit.

Personality theorist Gordon Allport calls this energy source the "propriate." To him this was the "motivational factor for the mature adult." It was his word for ego or self; it comprised the "core" of personality. To Allport there must be an essence of life from which energy originates. Psychoanalytic founder Sigmund Freud called this quality of life the "instinct." He assumed that functions of the body were done through "psychic energy." He stated, "The human instinct is the basic unit of personality. It is the motivation, the propelling force of personality that not only drives behavior but also determines its direction." I contend that these personality theorists are defining the biblical concept of spirit, the essence of life within us.

(2) <u>The human spirit can be characterized.</u> I delight in teaching this at college. I have the students take out a small piece of paper and then they turn the paper back to me nameless. I challenge them "to characterize themselves in one word." I collect the papers and before the class in animated fashion conjure students who have put a "negative" word on the paper. I extol those who have put down positive words such as loving, happy, cheerful, or optimistic. Now come on... how do some people get so negative, and others are positive? What word would you use to characterize your spirit?

I challenge you to write that word down: _____

We characterize people through their spirit. When I was in seminary, I pastored a small, local church. After my first sermon, I was greeting people at the door. To a particular lady (now deceased), I made the mistake of inquiring, "How are you today?" As she complained, I contend, she gave to me an "organ recital." (She related what was wrong with each of her organs... you will forgive me?) I learned never to ask again. Now don't misunderstand... the using of this illustration does not mean that we should not be understanding and loving to hurting people. However, we must not only be able to step back and analyze the human spirit, but we must understand the "etiology" of such.

The Bible speaks of "haughty" spirits (Prov. 16:18) and of "humble and contrite spirits" (Isa. 66:2). Proverbs l7: 27 states, "He that hath knowledge sparesh his words and a man of understanding is of an <u>excellent</u> spirit." [Emphasis added] The Hebrew word here is *yagar*, which among possible rendering is the word "cool." It doesn't quite follow teenage vernacular, but it does have an "awesome" meaning. It implies that when others are upset and when circumstances are confusing, there is at least one person who is "under control." His furnace is not heated up. He is "cool." Are you getting excited yet? Let's take it a step further. In 1 Peter 3:4, the Christian wife is exhorted to have a "gentle and quiet spirit." The Greek word for "quiet" can be translated as "mild, tranquil, or peaceable." Here is a lady who can sustain a cool, quiet spirit in the face of adversity. Let's all accept the challenge to learn from this material and become a "cool" person.

(3) <u>We worship and learn in the spirit.</u> John 4:24 states, "God is a Spirit, and they that worship Him must worship in spirit and in truth." This passage relates that change is dependent upon attitude. I can go to church and not really be there in "spirit." I can go to school and not be a student. If at school I do not have an attitude to learn and to study, I will not change or grow.

I recall dramatically an incident that occurred toward the conclusion of my master's degree program. A professor, being a bit of a "free spirit," decided to pull two students to the front of the class and let the rest of the class "analyze" them. This was at a secular university. I knew when he introduced this project that I would be chosen (and I was). The students were encouraged to make various observations about the other student and myself. When my classmates had finished their observations, the professor decided to make his comments. He began (with a smile), "Duane, your biggest problem is that you came to this class not as a student but as a teacher. I will tell you how you have given yourself away. When you ask questions of me, you preface them with the words, 'don't you think' or 'don't you agree?' You are not asking me questions; you are trying to manipulate me into your conclusion." I will never, never forget those comments. At the ripe old age of twenty-three, I was not a student. Are you still a student? Can others correct you? We all can be shocked by our own self-deception.

(4) <u>The human spirit is the first point of change.</u> The teacher shook the little boy adamantly and pushed him down into the chair. The boy's face coiled with rebellion and glaring, he responded, "In my body I am sitting down, but in my spirit, I am still standing up." People must have a desire to change. Bless you. You have purchased this book. Do you really want to deal with your anger and your argumentative spirit? Do you want to become a different person? It has to start within the spirit. How motivated are you to change? Could I encourage you to assimilate this material analytically and not critically? Now, how is the spirit connected with the soul?

I am going to attempt to prove that the human spirit and human soul are both unified and distinct. They work separate and together. They are both involved within an argumentative person. Are you confused yet? Hold on.

As an example, in the Old Testament the Hebrew word *nephesh*, which is translated both spirit and soul, is used some 171 times. Basically, but not inclusively, the word relates to the life principle in both animals and humans (Gen. 1:20, 24). This would be consistent with our spirit. At times, however, this word is translated "soul" and it is equated to human personality. In Proverbs 13:4, it relates that the soul can desire, "…the soul of a lazy man desires and has nothing…." Let's consider three basic principles of the soul.

(1) The spirit and the soul are distinct. There are a number of passages that explore this uniqueness. In the Old Testament, Isaiah 26:9 states, "…with my soul have I desired thee in the night; yet with my spirit within me will I seek thee early." Please note that it is the soul that desires and it is the spirit that seeks. We will return to this thought later. In the New Testament, Luke 1:46-47, Mary during her pregnancy with Jesus commented, "my soul doeth magnify the Lord, and my spirit hath rejoiced in God my Savior." We have already suggested that there are three distinct words in the Greek for the spirit (*pneuma*), the soul (*psychos*), and the body (*sarkas*). The preceding verses note the "interaction" within the spirit/ soul, but there can also be "interaction" within different parts of the soul. An example of this is Deuteronomy 4:9, "take heed, and keep thy soul diligently, lest you forget the things which thine eyes have seen… lest they depart from your heart." This is such an awesome passage relating how our memory and emotions are interacting within the soul. This has many ramifications. Note the distinction of parts of the soul with the wonder of the entire soul. Hold on.

(2) The soul, as the spirit, can be characterized. We know that the soul can be depressed. Did not Jonah cry unto the Lord to "please take my life" (Jon. 4:3). It can express anguish. David in Psalm 116:4 stated, "Oh Lord, I implore you, deliver my soul." The soul can be bitter. Job wailed in Job 3:20, "Wherefore is light given to him that is in misery, and life

unto the bitter in soul." We will explore this momentarily, but realize that if my soul is bitter; the tendency will be for me to interpret most everything in life with bitterness. I don't drink coffee (blessings on all your coffee drinkers). To me the taste of coffee is bitter (taste buds on my tongue). I believe it to be bitter. I have reinforced that it is bitter. Why would I ever consider drinking a substance that I have already interpreted to be bitter? As adults, we have interpretative thoughts from our soul about most all things.

If you had to characterize your soul in one word what would it be? _____

Perhaps Jacob's condemnation of his sons Simeon and Levi is the best example of anger (Gen. 49:5-7) coming from the soul. He wanted to be sure that his "soul" did not enter their counsel. These two sons were described as being cruel (v. 5). They were so angry and so cruel that they killed a man and lamed an ox. Verse seven states, "cursed be their anger, for it was fierce, and their wrath, for it was cruel." Note that others were observing these personality manifestations in them. When others observe us are we "cool" or are we argumentative?

(3) <u>The soul is the interpretive part of our personality.</u> As I imply above, if the spirit is the furnace, it is the soul that interprets. Note that in the structure presented in the last chapter, we suggested that our soul has five parts: the memory, the will, the intellect, faith energy, and our emotions. All of these have interpretive features. We can remember and interpret past experiences. We can love or laugh; we can interpret a joke as being humorous. Even now as you are thinking with me, you are interpreting. You are responding

in a positive or negative way to this material. At the college I relate to the students that they can not only be bored, but also they can know that they are bored. I relate, "Ah… the profoundness of being bored."

It is has long been my contention that it is not what happens to us, but it is how we interpret it. No person, no situation, no circumstance is anymore of a threat to us than what we make it. As we move toward the "healing" of our argumentative spirit, this interpretive phase within us must profoundly and dramatically be altered. The will becomes the rudder for change.

In reflection, I have learned much from wise, older people. Mrs. Almstrom (now deceased) had arthritis so badly she could hardly walk. But she attended every church function. On Sunday mornings, she and other "elder" folk had Sunday school on the first level of the church. For the worship service she had to climb steep stairs to the sanctuary. For Mrs. Almstrom this was painful. She grimaced with each step. One Sunday I met her at the top of the steps (she refused to let me help her), and stated, "That must be awfully painful." Her response was, "Oh no, oh no, pastor you must realize that it is not my pain, it is God's pain. He is only giving to me the privilege of feeling it." It is never what happens to us; it is always how we interpret it.

A good example of this would be the principle in Proverbs 22:5, "Thorns and snares are in the way of the perverse; he who guards his soul will be far from them." Notice how the "soul" is aware of the temptation and the distortion, but it is protected. The soul is the "seat of our appetites." Psalms 107:9 relates that "God satisfies the longing soul and fills the hungry soul…." Do you have any longings that you want filled? The soul is also the "seat of our minds." Deuteronomy 26:16 states, "The Lord your God commands you to observe these statutes and judgment; therefore, be careful to observe them with all your heart and with all your soul."

(4) <u>God desires "perfection" in our spirit and soul.</u> As we have stated, one of God's goals for us is perfection. Passages such as Hebrews 12:23, Job 9:21, and James 1:4 make clear that God wants us to become "perfect and entire, wanting nothing." As we are struggling with flesh on any level, we have choices as to how we interpret the struggles in our life and how we feed our soul.

Indeed the spirit and the soul are both separate and together. I have both a furnace (energy source), and I have an interpretive phase in my being. Basically, it is the spirit that "feeds" the soul, but it is the soul that interprets. I am amazed that energy can be pushed through me, interpreted, and expressed through my body. I am doing that as I write. Let me illustrate a bit more dramatically. I can be driving my car on a beautiful day, when suddenly another car can cut in front of me. My spirit reacts. My soul interprets. My body responds. They all work simultaneously but each plays a part in accomplishing the task of my survival. Note that the soul is the most important because it is there that I interpret. I have options. I can respond, "God bless that driver; he must be in a hurry. I want to get out of his way; so I don't slow him down." Or another option might be, "That x###**zzxx guy. Does he think he owns the road?" Is your soul cool or impulsive? Here is one more illustration for those of you that are married. Your spouse corrects you. Do you respond, "Well thank you honey. Thank you for calling to my attention this small idiosyncrasy." Or do you respond, "How dare you correct me when you have so many glaring faults?"

Obviously, in dealing with argumentation, the soul must be reconditioned in the interpreting of our life experiences.

Jesus gives to us an awesome example of this in the Sermon on the Mount (Matt. 5-7). He states that if someone hits us on our right cheek, we should turn to him the other cheek also (5:39). Certainly, this is the way most of us would respond. "You have given to me a right, black eye, please would you match that on the left eye?" Most of us would need quite a metamorphous to have this interpretation.

However, perhaps Jesus' most profound thought was in Matthew 5:41. He states that if someone "compels to go a mile, go with him two." Israel was under bondage to the Roman Empire at this time. Laws had been passed that required Jewish citizens to carry goods of Roman soldiers a mile if ordered to do so. If they refused, the penalty could be death. Let's get this in perspective. As of this writing, the United States has declared war on terrorism. We went to Afghanistan and fought against a radical Islamic group called the Taliban. They were defeated and a democratic government was put into place in that country. Let's suppose that we had lost that war. Let's suppose that the Taliban had not only won, but they came to this country, and they passed laws that said that we had to carry if requested their goods a

CHAPTER FOUR

ARGUMENTATIVE PEOPLE ARE SICK–DEFENDED

Anger and argumentation are correlated. When our opinions are challenged, why do we have to retort? Why do we have to be right? Proverbs 16:32 states, "He that is slow to anger is better than the mighty, and he that ruleth his spirit than he that taketh a city" [Emphasis added]. At the close of this material, you will be able to rule your spirit. How many arguments have you had in your life? If you had a quarter for every argument you have had in my life, and you were going to make travel plans accordingly, how far around the world could you go? I have heard my wife say many times, "You have to have the last word, don't you?" She is right. There is "something" in my spirit and soul that is triggered during a confrontation. As someone is talking, I am thinking rebuttal. I am thinking, "Go ahead and finish and I will tell you where you are wrong."

It starts with my sin nature. We must recognize that because of our sin nature, we have a force within us that is capable of controlling us, reigning over us, and using us as instruments of unrighteousness. Psalms 51:1-2 states, "Have mercy on me, O God, according to thy lovingkindness, according unto the multitude of thy tender mercies, blot out my transgressions, wash me thoroughly from mine iniquity and cleanse me from my sin." As previously stated, we determined that our sin nature has at least three parts. The word "sin" means that we have "missed the mark." The word "iniquity" means that we are "bent away from God." Our argumentative spirit comes from the word translated "transgression." The Hebrew word is *pesha*. We are in a "state of rebellion." It is much easier to be negative than positive and argumentative than quiet. It is within our very nature.

This has been reinforced through our genetic predisposition. Some of us are more "predisposed" to arguing and anger. As previously stated, we know from Psalm 139 that God has placed the "bent" within each child. Of the four basic temperaments, irritable, defiant, sensitive, and compliant, the irritable and defiant people are more prone to anger. However, a sensitive or compliant person, whose "spirits" have been crushed (Prov. 15:4), can become strong-willed, and they can become "fighters." Intuitively they think, "I have taken enough." They individualize. They change. The irony is that many times the instigator does not understand, and the argumentation becomes more intense.

It is reinforced by my gender. Studies relate that men generally are more argumentative then women. Dr. Mark Cogsgrove in his article, "The Anger Difference," comments,

> Brain differences between the sexes can lead men and women to view anger-producing situation with different mindsets. These same brain differences can also predispose men and women to choose certain responses to anger rather than others. In general, women are more likely to display a wider range of emotion in anger than are men. This does not just mean that women cry more when angry, which they do. Women are also more likely than men to verbalize their angers and reasons for their angers. Men on the other hand are more likely than women to be aggressive in anger situations are.

Dr. Cogsgrove gives three reasons that men and women differ in their expressions of anger: (1) brain differences; (2) hormonal differences; and (3) social differences. He continues...

> Recent studies reveal that female brains are "net like" in that they show more elaborate connections in all cortical areas. The female also has a proportionately larger corpus callosum than the male, which also increases emotional and verbal interconnections in all areas of the female brain. Male brains by contrast... have less circuitry connecting the centers. One result

of such brain differences is that the female brain seems more personal and detail oriented. The male brain, by contrast, offers a less personal, more abstract view of the world. It is easier for the male to see people as objects... that may lead him into acts of greater violence and aggression. Women by contrast are more likely to use their verbal superiority than muscles to attack, and they will continue arguments internally long after confrontations.

Higher male hormonal levels are also implicated in male aggressiveness and more overt expressions of anger... the male hormone testerone is implicated in this. Men generally have 10 times the level of testosterone in their bodies than women have.... Both sexes get angry but the flood of testosterone in males pushes harder against men toward certainly more anger expressions.... Although a flood of testosterone does not guarantee aggression and anger, it does provide the rush of energy that males can use for aggressive purposes.

Society also conditions or at least reinforces already existing biological differences between men and women. Our culture does in some ways free the male to engage in more overtly aggressive anger. Women, who feel just as angry, learn to show less direct expressions of anger. Society often expects little girls to be nice and sweet and never angry. Society may not encourage aggressive displays in young males, but aggression is more discouraged in young females. Society, therefore, reinforces some of the natural inclinations of men and women with regard to external aggression verses verbal and indirect expressions of anger.

Thus, it starts with a "triggering" within our spirits. No one starts out with a life ambition of becoming a drunk, or a prostitute, or an argumentative person. Most struggles are progressive. The person who starts with social drinking does not perceive himself as a drunk. The person begins with a basic curiosity, but one day finds himself entrenched in pornography. In this evolutionary process there is a "triggering" mechanism. Somewhere the struggles become both obsessive and compulsive. Thus, I believe that mental sickness goes through five stages: (1) We have a sin nature predisposed for our demise; (2) We become self-centered; (3) We become defensive; (4) We "trigger" mental sickness; and (5) We reinforce this sickness. Now remember "self-realization" is the first step of change.

Let's consider the etiology (source) of "argumentative" sick people. It has two steps:

<u>People with an argumentative spirit have a "fractured spirit."</u> Throughout this phase of our study, we will analyze the word contention in the Scriptures. Romans 2:6 relates that, "God will render to every man according to his deeds. To them who by patient continuance (persistence) in well doing seek for glory and honour an immortality, eternal life. <u>But unto them that are</u> <u>contentious</u> and do not obey the truth, but obey unrighteousness, indignation, and wrath. Tribulation

and anguish upon every soul of man that does evil of the Jew first and also of the Gentile. But glory, honor, and peace, to every man that worketh well, to the Jew first, and also to the Gentile. For there is no respect of persons with God." [Emphasis added]

The Greek work for "contention" here is *erithera,* which among possible translations, is a "fractured spirit." Now if that seems a bit abstract, remember that in the study of DID (Dissociative Identity Disorders), studies have shown that patients can not only have different personalities within them, but that each of these personalities can have his/her own memory patterns. (This disorder was formerly called MPD or multiple personality disorder.) In this disorder the memory becomes split or fractured. My premise is that this can also happen to the human spirit.

It gets a bit more ironic in that there is already a disease called "erethism" taken from this Greek word. It basically refers to an individual who has "morbid energy, hyper, and restless." Mercury toxicity can also lead to this diagnosis. Among the symptoms manifested is irritability, outbursts of temper, and stress intolerance. It also relates to the sexual effects of certain drugs upon some individuals. This can lead to a hyper alertness and hyper sexuality.

Now folks, when you get as old as I am, you can take certain liberties. In my judgment the psychological and physiological communities at this point have missed it. The theological community has it correct. The word is translated "contentious." There has been a "fracturing" within the spirit that has led to an illness. People who argue are indeed sick. The spirit was separated into component parts. Let's consider, scripturally, some of the manifestations of this illness.

(1) <u>The spirit can be agitated</u>. Proverbs 15:13 states, "A merry heart maketh a cheerful countenance, but by sorrow of heart the spirit is broken (agitated)." The Hebrew word literally means to "smite" or "afflict"—an instant sharp pain. Lewis Smedes in his book, *The Art of Forgiving,* discusses two types of hurts. The first one he calls the hurt of "disloyalty." He defines this as "when someone who belongs to you treats you like a stranger." Have you ever felt slighted, or abandoned, or neglected? How did this affect your spirit? Did it "color" your attitudes of trust or confidence? The second hurt Dr. Smedes calls the hurt of "betrayal." During this stage individuals choose to "cut you into pieces." Have you ever had anyone turn on you with such force that you were "cut to pieces?" How did it affect you?

(2) <u>The spirit can be wounded.</u> Proverbs 18:14 states, "The spirit of a man will sustain his infirmity, but a wounded spirit, who can bear it?" This is the same Hebrew word from above, but it is in a more intense form. Through counseling for over thirty years, I have heard many stories. I will not soon forget a young lady relating how her alcoholic father, pulled to the floor a meal that her mother had prepared, and in the presence of the children, grabbed his wife by the back of the neck and made her eat the food from the floor. Can we conjuncture the possible effects of this upon the children? What did they feel? What did they think about marriage, relationships, and love? Would it wound the spirit?

(3) <u>The spirit can be crushed.</u> Proverbs 15:4 says, "A wholesome tongue is a tree of life but perverseness therein is a breach [crushes] the spirit." This is a much stronger word, meaning to break, crush, or even destroy. I had a cousin who was captured by the Chinese in the Korean War. He was in captivity for some two years, and during that time, his spirit was crushed. Before going into the service, he was a happy, jovial individual. After the war he became a quiet, solemn individual. I remember asking him, "What happened?" He related that if I had gone through what he had experienced, I would not be the same either. I don't doubt some of you have had experiences so traumatic that your spirit has been crushed.

4) <u>The spirit can become haughty.</u> Proverbs 16:18 relates, "Pride goeth before destruction and a haughty spirit before the fall." The Hebrew word for haughty means "lofty and prideful." The individual can't be told anything. I recall a counseling situation in which the husband would not let the wife talk. He would literally not let her finish a sentence without interrupting and "correcting" her.

5) <u>The spirit can become argumentative.</u> Proverbs 29:1 states, "He that being often reproved hardens his neck, shall suddenly be destroyed and that without remedy." The word "hardens," means the individual becomes stiff-necked and unmovable. He has regressed intuitively to the point that no matter what the issue, he/she is ready to counter and be argumentative.

A lady came to a counseling session intent on changing her husband. She assaulted him openly during the first session. He sat quietly; realizing any attempted retort would be futile. I opened the second session by relating that I would not be meeting with them further. "But why," she demanded. "Well," I retorted, "if we continue counseling, Mrs. ____ , I will eventually have to relate that you are part of the problem, and you will not respond well. So it is best for us to discontinue now." She immediately got up, agreed with me, took her husband's hand and left. People with argumentative spirits generally are not open to correction. This topic will eventually be discussed. Who corrects you? How do you respond?

(6) <u>The spirit can become closed.</u> There is not a definite passage here, but I do think of the contention between Paul and Barnabus over Mark in Acts 15:24-41. Verse 39 relates that the contention was so sharp between them that they departed asunder one from the other. Gary Smalley, in his book *The Key to Your Child's Heart,* has a good chapter on parents and children closing off their spirits from one another. On any level this could be a natural progression of the other "syndromes" discussed. If the irritation is so intense that the spirit is agitated, wounded, and crushed, the tendency might be to close off our spirit or to posture to fight back. We become argumentative.

So let's review. If we have been wounded or crushed in our spirit, it is possible we have developed an argumentative spirit. We are calling the disease "erethism" taken from the Greek word translated "contentious." The very essence of life within us, our spirit, has become "fractured" and splintered. A "perceived attack" will "trigger" the disorder and we become angry, enraged, resentful, or indignant.

Thus, our spirit might intuitively function accordingly.

The second phase of the illness is the effect upon the soul. Remember, the soul is our "interpretive" part. Right now... as you are reading... you are interpreting. Proverbs 13:18 is such an awesome passage: "A desire accomplished is sweet to the soul...." Think with me of a "desire" that you accomplished. Remember your first house... your college degree... that special car. How did you feel? Notice that your soul was "sweet." The word literally means "pleasurable." You know when you are happy compared to when you are sad. Conversely, Proverbs 27:7 states, "A satisfied soul loathes the honeycomb, but to a hungry soul every bitter thing is sweet." The hungry soul tries to "cover" the bitterness. Perhaps if I get drunk enough... high enough... angry enough but the bitterness is still there.

Your wounded spirit has affirmed a persona (a personality). How did you obtain this personality? Would others consider you positive, optimistic, loving, and happy? Or would others consider you negative, pessimistic, self-centered, and sad? I contend that your spirit has fed your soul. The constructs of your soul have become set. Whether positive or negative, you have become predictable. Your spouse and family can anticipate your anger and argumentation.

Again, let's review our study of the word "contentious." The Hebrew word in the Old Testament is *midyar* (erithera in Greek New Testament) which among meanings is translated "ill tempered...." Note the use of the word ill. Our premise is that "people who argue are sick." Here are a couple of examples. Proverbs 21:19, "I is better to dwell in the wilderness, than

with a <u>contentious and angry woman."</u> [Emphasis added]
You know these people when you meet them. They are "ill"
tempered. When I was a child, I lived near a contentious
woman. She stood "guard" by her home, and if any person's
foot touched her lawn, she was out "growling." Tragically,
kids being who they are, and the sin nature being what it is,
her property took a beating. I genuinely felt bad for her at
Halloween. Men also can be "ill" tempered. Proverbs 26:21
states, "As coals are to burning coals, and wood to fire, so is
a <u>contentious man to kindle strife."</u> [Emphasis added] Let's
remember that it is the fathers who are exhorted in Ephesians
6:4 not to "provoke our children to wrath." I remember a
man during a counseling session relating that he would "pull"
the spark plug wires in the car to keep his wife from going
to church.

Let's consider four "personality types" that can be formed
from a person sick with the disease *erethism*. These are four
"ill tempered" souls of people who have experienced fractured
spirits. Check if any of these would describe you.

<u>The Callused Person</u>—(the indifferent person). This
perhaps would come from a "wounded" person. Have you
been wounded in your life? Have you defensively become
callused as a result? This person can be very argumentative.
Proverbs 15:1 states, "A soft answer turneth away wrath, but
<u>grievous words"</u> stir up anger." The Hebrew word here is *etseb*.
It means to be hurtful and to "inflict pain." The speaker of
these "grievous words" wants to see the other person hurting.
Another place where the word is used is Proverbs 15:18, "A
wrathful man stirreth up strife, but he that is slow to anger

appeaseth strife." How much are you oblivious to the hurts of others? Early in my marriage I remember how insensitive I was to my wife's crying. Please Father forgive me. The number one criteria for mental health is to see the problem from the other's perspective. For the callused person this is very difficult.

The Crushed Person–(the sarcastic person)–This perhaps comes from an individual whose spirit has been crushed. Is your initial impulse to retort sarcastically? Proverbs 15:4 says, "A wholesome tongue is a tree of life but perversion is a breach (crushing) of the spirit." The word perversion means "out of focus." A person with a crushed spirit is either quiet or responds back with cynicism. As previously stated, this might be especially true of a sensitive person. If we return to our discussion of temperaments, I would classify myself as irritable (type A) and my wife as sensitive. You can appreciate that with the strength of my personality in the early days of our marriage, I crushed the spirit of my wife. She is wonderful, loving, caring, and compassionate, but... after a few years of this, she began to resist. I had crushed her spirit and brought out her will to fight back.

While dining with perhaps my best friend, I was asked, "Duane, what do you perceive to be my worst character flaw?" (Talk about wrecking a good lunch.) I responded, "Lou, do you really want my assessment?"

"Yes, he retorted, "perhaps it would be a help to me."

"Well Lou," since you asked, "your worse character flaw is that you are a cynic. No matter what is discussed, your initial (triggering) response, is to be critical. You have become a cynic." Notice please… all of us have become something. We all have a persona (personality).

The Contentious Person–(the nagging person)–This perhaps is the result of the development of an argumentative spirit. Proverbs 17:14 says, "The beginning of strife is as when one lets out water; therefore, leave off contention, before it be meddled with…." This is a different Hebrew word (*riyh*). This is a quarreling and disputing person. Your initial "triggering" response to contention is to become aggressive, vociferous, and direct. This Scripture gives us a good analogy. Imagine watering your lawn, and then trying to get the water back through the hose. You can't be a quarreling person without experiencing consequences. You will see them in your spouse and in your children. We wonder why our children argue so much without realizing that we have modeled this for them.

The Chafed Person–(the offended person)–This perhaps is the person with the closed spirit. Proverbs 18:19 relates that, "The brother offended [stepped on] is harder to be won than a strong city, and their contentions are like the bars of a castle." I think of a patient who was punished as a child by being locked in his room for weeks. Food was literally shoved through the door. This same person as an adult came home from work one day and found a note from his wife relating that she had left. In his mind he loved his wife, but he seldom talked with her. Even in counseling he had such a difficult time expressing his feelings. Many times he would just sit and cry. He could not talk. Anger, however, had seeped into his soul. My heart hurt for him.

Thus, your crushed, wounded, and/or closed spirit (*erethism*) has affected your soul. You have become cynical, or contentious, or chafed without even realizing the depth of your sickness. You have indeed become ill tempered. Your soul has taken on a negative persona. Others will observe this even if you do not. But a sovereign God had you begin reading this book because He wants to heal you. Getting excited yet? The steps of my own healing have been incredible. We will consider the consequences of this sickness for a couple chapters, investigate how this anger is expressed, and then we will begin, by God's grace, the healing process. So hold on.

Let's close the chapter with a test.

Let's test ourselves. Rate yourself 1-10 (ten the highest). Add your totals and grade accordingly: 90-100—A, 80-89—B, 70-79—C, 60-69—D, Below 60—F.

1. Would others consider you an argumentative person?
   _____

2. Have you been hurt and wounded in the past?
   _____

3. Have you forgiven those who have given you pain?
   _____

4. Would you consider yourself a strong-willed person?
   _____

5. Do you have a tendency to overact to small problems?
   _____

6. Did your parents argue excessively?

   _____

7. Do you generally "want to continue" an argument?

   _____

8. Have you had "crushing" experiences in your past?

   _____

9. Have you ever "struck" your spouse, children, or others in anger?

   _____

10. Do you "internalize" your anger at times?

    _____

Total _____Score _____

CHAPTER FIVE

SATAN SNARES
THE SPIRIT/SOUL

B efore eventually suggesting steps of healing, I want to explore with you some of the effects of this "fractured" spirit and "ill tempered" soul. This chapter will deal with Satan's attempts to exploit this sickness, and the next chapter will explore how our argumentative spirit can become transgenerational. It is sobering to realize that we can now be affecting potential grandchildren.

Matthew 5:37 is a sobering verse. It states, "But let your communication be yea, yea, nay, nay, for <u>whatsoever is more than these cometh of evil (from the evil one)</u>" [Emphasis added] This refers to Satan. Satan is not sovereign, but through his hordes of demons, he can identify our weaknesses. And dearly beloveds, he attacks. He becomes conscious of our struggles, and he exploits them. Athletics are built around the same premise. As a former football and basketball player (oh so many years ago), I recall that you were constantly analyzing where your opponents were perceived to be vulnerable. Proverbs 7 gives to us an analogy of a prostitute, which shows how Satan operates: she entices a young man, she sets the trap, she teases, she lies, and finally the young man is caught. The 22nd verse begins, "He goes after her straightway, as an ox goes to the slaughter... as a bird hastes to a snare, and knoweth not that it is for his life... for she hath <u>cast down many wounded</u>; yea, many strong men <u>have been slain by her</u>" [Emphasis added] I trust you caught that. He is wounded; he is vulnerable, and the devil is waiting to pounce. 1 Peter 5:8 exhorts us to "be sober, be vigilant, because your adversary the devil, as a roaring lion, walks about, seeking whom he may devour." The word for "devour" is "swallow," and let's quickly note that Peter is writing to Christians. His comments are directed to either or both of the following: (1) some Christians who have already met the fate of being consumed; and/or (2) others who are ready to be consumed by their enemy, and Peter is warning of this.

When Peter in Matthew 16:22, "rebuked Jesus"... that's rebuked... rebuked <u>Jesus</u>, Jesus responded to Peter, "Get thee behind me Satan...." Peter was striving to discourage Jesus from Calvary and His ultimate crucifixion on the cross for our sins. Jesus immediately recognized that this was from Satan; however, the words were flowing from Peter's mouth.

Satan can and will use our words in his attempt to destroy us. Second Corinthians, chapter two, addresses dissention over a brother in the church at Corinth. Paul exhorts the church to "confirm" their love for that brother...." Verse eight warns, "lest Satan should get an advantage of us, for we are not ignorant of his devices." The Greek word for "advantage" not only denotes "to get gain" but also to "twine or braid" us. Note how Satan is striving to utilize situations in our lives to bind and strangle us.

And now we are ready for the passage in Ephesians 4:26-27 that directly deals with Satan utilizing our argumentative spirit to get a "foothold" in our lives. The passage states, "Be ye angry, and sin not, let not the sun go down upon your wrath. <u>Neither give place to the devil."</u> The word for place means to "get a position" or "to get a home." Can it be any more obvious? Those of us who have argued into the night, have opened ourselves up directly to demonic activity and inhabitation. And again, let's remember that this is written to the church. Praise God. We have no angry people in our churches, do we? Amen.

The Bible gives to us a grotesque image of the devil and his demons. We know that Satan was at one time an angel in heaven (Ezek. 28:11-19; Isa. 14:12-14; Job 38:1-7). At one point in the past, he attempted to lead a rebellion in heaven against God (Rev. 12:7). He was defeated and the earth was given to him as his domain. He became the God of this world (Eph. 2:2; 2 Cor. 4:4). In Satan's fall, he drew a vast number of angels with him (Rev. 12:4, 9). Some of the fallen angels are loose and some are bound in a place called the Abyss (Luke 8:31). The loose ones we call "demons," or evil spirits. Of the bound ones, there are two kinds: permanently bound (2 Pet. 2:4; Jude 6) and temporarily bound (Rev. 9:1-11). Satan and his demons now wage war against God's kingdom (Rev. 12:17). We know that demons can enter both people and animals (Luke 4 and Luke 8). In the story of "legion" in Luke, chapter 8, we know that the man was possessed with many evil spirits. We know that Satan is devoid of conscience and he is a liar (John 8:44). And unlike what is portrayed by Hollywood, demons can appear in attractive forms. Demons are deceivers. They love to masquerade. Paul wrote to the Corinthians and said that their church at Corinth had eagerly received evil spirits into their midst (2 Cor. 11:4) in the form of false prophets and false apostles. Paul warned them that even "Satan himself masquerades as an angel of light. It is not surprising, then, that his servants masquerade as ministers of righteousness" (2 Cor. 11:14-15).

We know from the Scriptures that Satan tempts believers to disobedience:

(1 Chron. 21:1-7), to lose faith in God (Luke 22:31-32; l Pet. 5:8), to lie (Acts 5:32), to be immoral (1 Cor. 7:5), to be preoccupied by the world (1 John 2:15; 2 Tim. 4:10), to be proud (1 Tim. 3:6), and to be discouraged (1 Pet. 5:6, 7, 10).

Do we understand this demonization process? Merrill Unger in his book, *Demons in the World Today*, said "demonization is a condition in which one or more spirits or demons inhabit the body of a human being and can take complete control of their victim at will. By temporarily blotting out consciousness, they can speak and act through him as their complete slave or tool. The inhabiting demon (or demons) comes and goes much like the proprietor of a house who may or may not be 'at home'". He may precipitate an attack. In these attacks the victim passes from his normal state, in which he acts like other people, to an abnormal state...."

Dearly beloved, this battle is real. For fourteen years I directed a Youth for Christ chapter in Ann Arbor, Michigan. One day I received a call from the director of Campus Crusade at the University of Michigan. "Duane," he said, "I need to ask you a question. What experiences have you had with demons?"

"Well," I replied, "not much. I had some instruction in my theology class in seminary, but that is about it."

He continued, "I have a young lady that I strongly suspect is demonically possessed, and I need some help to verify this. Will you help?"

I responded favorably; so on a crisp November day, he brought this young lady to my office. She had graduated from King's College in New York, and she had come to the University of Michigan to pursue a Master's degree in music. She had a strong, religious background. We eventually discovered that some two years previously, over a two-week period she had three compelling, traumatic experiences. She was "dropped" by her boyfriend, and her father was killed in a hunting accident, and her brother was killed in a car accident. Seemingly these events led to her total disorientation.

My office was in a small house; so the Campus Crusade director chose to wait outside in the car.

The young lady and I talked briefly, and then I suggested that I pray with her. She was sitting in a soft, cushioned chair and I was in front of her in a metal chair. Among the mistakes that I made in dealing with her was to hold her wrists with my hands. As I started into the prayer, I compelled any "evil spirits" that were within to identify themselves and leave her in Jesus' name. At this point in the prayer she shook and went into a seizure. I was not sure what I was doing, but what I now perceive to be the Holy Spirit within me started shouting at the evil spirits that indwelled her. In a few seconds the seizure subsided. Still holding her wrists, I related that we were going to do it again, and identically at the same point in the prayer, again she went into a seizure. At this point, again I began shouting, and suddenly a voice came from within her that said, "Leave her alone, she is mine." There was a brief dialogue in which the demons argued that she did not want them to leave. The girl was shaking. Then suddenly she went limp. Motivation overwhelmed reason. I began this a third time. As I started the prayer, suddenly this girl took on great power, and with my hands on the "top" of her wrists, I was lifted off the floor in my chair, and I was thrown against the wall. I was not hurt. The girl bolted from the house, ran past the car, and continued about a half mile down the road, and there she collapsed. This incident did wonders for my theology. I must have immediately read a dozen books on this subject. I am happy to relate that I drew other people into this situation and eventually six demons were released from within her.

Another incident impacted my theology. Ron was a good friend both in high school and college. It was my privilege to room with him two years in college. Ron claimed that he had an aunt in Pennsylvania who could tell the future. She was a Christian lady. Well, I was very young at the time, and I was very skeptical. However, two incidents occurred during my high school years that "piqued" my curiosity. Ron's father was involved in an accident. The family was concerned about medical expenses, but the aunt "prophesied" that they would receive a large sum of money, which they did. His father also was diagnosed with cancer, and he was not expected to live. The aunt in Pennsylvania "prophesied" that the doctors were wrong and that he would live a full life, which he did. Ron was close to failing at the end of his sophomore year. He contacted this aunt, and she said that he would finish college, which he did. I related to Ron that if this lady ever came for a visit, I would like to meet her. That happened, and still as a very young man, I queried her, "From where do you get this power?" Now please understand that I am convinced that she is a fine, Christian lady." Her answer, I will never forget. She related, "God has given to me the power to discern the spirits. There are many spirits in this world, both good and bad, and the most prominent good spirit is the Holy Spirit, that comes directly from God. But there are also many good and evil spirits in any setting."

This thought is reinforced in 1 John 4:1, where we are exhorted to "try the spirits," testing whether they are of God. Note that this is plural. And the next verse continues, "Hereby know ye the Spirit [Holy Spirit] of God; every spirit that confesseth that Jesus Christ is come in the flesh is of God." Now help me folks. Is the implication not that there are other "good spirits" besides the Holy Spirit? This could be interpreted as the "spirits" of individuals or as other "detached" spirits. But let's continue into the next verse, "And every spirit that confesseth not that Jesus Christ is come in the flesh is not of God, and this is that anti-christ, whereof ye have heard that it should come, and even now is already in the world." Note that the notion of "detached" spirits is reinforced, some good and some evil, and that the "spirit" of the anti-christ was active even in the first century.

Now we know from the Scriptures that God's Holy Spirit comes into our spirit. Jesus instructed Nicodemus in John 3:6, as he was striving to understand the new-birth experience, "that which is born of the flesh is flesh; and that which is born of the Spirit is spirit." Note the dynamics of the Holy Spirit and our spirit. Romans 8:16 relates that "the Spirit [Holy Spirit] itself beareth witness with our spirit [human spirit], that we are the children of God."

We are now ready to address the question, can evil spirits indwell believers? Partial defense for skeptics is the fourth verse of the 1 John 4 passage. It states, "ye are of God, little children, and have overcome them [evil spirits); <u>because greater is he that</u> <u>is in you, than he that is in the world."</u> As Christians, we do have the Holy Spirit within us, but this verse does not address whether evil spirits can also co-habitat the believer. We will eventually give you a theory.

We do have examples from the Scripture of "Christians" who became demon possessed. In the Old Testament the strongest example is King Saul. We know that Saul was a believer (1 Sam. 10:9). That passage relates that God changed Saul's heart. To argue that Saul was not a believer is to argue that God's Spirit would anoint an unbeliever (10:1), and that God would anoint an unbeliever to rule over the Jewish people. Furthermore, he was filled with the Spirit and prophesied (10:9-13). There appears here to be characteristics of a believer. Later, after sinning, he was tormented (demonized) by an evil spirit from the Lord (16:14). Note that God sent the evil spirit to Saul. Now folks, this implies many ramifications. God, obviously, can take control of evil spirits as He desires. We know that God can blind minds (2 Cor. 3:14 and Rom. 11:7) and God can give people over to reprobate (distorted) minds (Rom. 1:28). That should sober all of us a bit. Let's continue. The precise reason why Saul was invaded by a demon is nowhere directly indicated. It may have been that during his rebellion against God (1 Sam. 15:23), the door was opened for this evil spirit. You will note that when David would play his harp, the evil spirit would leave Saul (16:23).

The best examples in the New Testament were probably Ananias and Sapphira (Acts 5:1-11). It is assumed that Ananias and Sapphira were a part of the "believers" mentioned in Acts 4:32-35. Of course, in the dialogue, we know that they tried to hold back their giving from God. The Scripture tells us that Ananias had let Satan "fill" his heart. This is the same Greek word used in Ephesians 5:18 that challenges us as believers to be "filled" with the Holy Spirit. Seemingly, it has the same meaning here. Satan had control of Ananias, the believer, and caused him to lie to God.

There is an interesting passage in 1 Corinthians 5:1-5 of folk within the church of Corinth strongly engaged in fornication. Paul continues his comments concerning these people in verse five saying, "To deliver such an one unto Satan for the destruction of the flesh, that the spirit may be saved in the day of the Lord Jesus." Ramifications of this will be considered later.

So in reality, we today have many Christians experiencing vexing problems and struggles which go beyond natural psychological and emotional infirmities. At the request of her sister, many years ago I visited a bed-ridden lady who had a "tic" disorder. She was a graduate of Moody Bible Institute, and with pillows tied to her bed, as we talked about the Lord, she had both hands and feet flailing back and forth.

I previously mentioned a book by Merrill Unger, *Demons and the World Today*. In the book, he defended that Christians could be "oppressed" but not possessed. There was such an avalanche of dissent that he changed his mind. Among the dissenters was Dr. Raymond Edman, former president of Wheaton College. Dr. Edman had firsthand experience with crude demonism. He and his wife were former missionaries in Ecuador, and that gave to him an understanding of this subject sometimes not possessed by purely theoretical Bible interpreters. Dr. Unger rewrote the book under the title *What Demons Can Do to Saints*. In this book, he defended that Christians are vulnerable to demonic possession when the "believer's position in Christ is unguarded and the doors left wide open by flagrant disobedience and willful persistent sin." He continues, "Accordingly, Scripture clearly reveals that the believer is absolutely protected from Satan and demons in his 'position' before God in Christ by virtue of his salvation in Christ (Heb. 2:3). However, as far as his 'experience' is concerned protection against demonic attack is only proportionate as the believer knows and believes in his position and makes it his experience (Rom. 6:11)... similarly, in his position before God in Christ, the believer is a full panoplied soldier against whom Satan and demons are powerless. But, in his experience, Satan and demons can and will penetrate the armor unless the Christian warrior uses every part of it in resisting the enemy's attack (Eph. 6:10-18)...the situation may be compared to a man who owns a house. If he completely controls it and occupies it, no one, of course, can move in without his approval. But if he does not occupy all the rooms and is lax concerning who visits and how long they stay, he may soon find himself with an illegal dweller or two, who may prove very difficult to remove."

So Dr. Unger concluded that the Christian could be possessed. Demons could possess the body and the soul. He comments, "...through crass indulgence of the old nature, demon powers can influence through his body and soul. In cases where the sin is of such a character that it goes beyond the old nature, the demon may invade and cause upheaval and chaos in the believer through his body and soul. In this case, the child of God displays a kind of split personality. First he speaks and acts through the Spirit, but then under the influence of the demon power when it is in control."

Let's close the chapter with some hints of controversy. From my experience in the hand-full of situations where I have observed demon-possessed Christians, the spirit is also involved. There was no question that the very "essence of life," the furnace if you please, was also involved in the demonic expression. How is this possible? This is my theory. In the discussion of dissociative identity disorders, we suggested that many psychologists believe that when "alter personalities" are developed that each has its own memory bank. In this disorder the memory, if you please, is split. This is both complicated and intriguing. I think this is precisely what happens to the spirit of "demon controlled" Christians. In the last chapter we defended that during the development of "erethism," the human spirit splits. Taking it a step further, when the spirit is split, I content that evil spirits can indwell the believer in the "maladaptive" parts. Our passage in 1 Corinthians 5:5 says that the flesh was given over to Satan but the "spirit" was saved. The Holy Spirit will never totally be extracted, unless God, Himself, chooses to take the Holy Spirit from them. Part of the spirit is indwelt by evil spirits, and part of the spirit is indwelt by the Holy Spirit. Our works will be tested. We all eventually will face judgment. First Corinthians 3:15 states, "If any man's work shall be burned, he shall suffer loss, but he himself shall be saved; yet so as by fire." This implies, I know, that perhaps we will see Saul, Ananias and Sapphira, and perhaps even Judas in heaven. I want to strongly suggest that in my judgment that this demonization process is the exception and not the norm. Struggles I believe to be 90 percent psychological and 10 percent demonic. However, this does have strong ramifications for our sick, argumentative person.

I have already defended that the human spirit can be crushed, wounded, and weakened. I have already defended that the soul can became bitter and harsh. The devil can, through his demons, attack and eventually conquer and indwell the Christian. The argumentative spirit within us becomes more compelling and obsessive. The differences between the psychological and demonic are measured in the person's decorum, in his orientation, and in his intensity. Demon controlled people can become excessively vociferous.

Scripture does defend that "argumentation" and anger can affect both the spirit and the soul. Ecclesiastes 7:9 challenges us, "do not hasten your spirit to be angry, for anger rests in the <u>bosom</u> of fools." The Hebrew word for "bosom" means "within" the person. This would be consistent with our emotions, our will, and our soul. Proverbs 22:24-25 states, "...and with a furious man thou shalt not go, lest you learn his ways, and get a snare to your soul." I started this chapter with the words "it's sobering...." Dearly beloved, it is sobering to realize that not only can we become sick and develop erethism, but that a spirit of anger and argumentation can indwell us and we can become demonized.

CHAPTER SIX

ARGUMENTATIVE SPIRIT—
Trans-generational Curses

I n psychology we call it "measured effects." Can we begin to calculate the effects of having an argumentative spirit? As a child, I met my grandfather Cuthbertson just once. I remember how angry he seemed. My response was to pull back from him. My father had an argumentative spirit. But Dad, God blessed him as he got older and this subsided. He died at ninety-three.

The effects of an argumentative spirit run deep. The question does arise, "Are we coded by God transgenerationally?" Psalms 139 in relating how God "fashioned" us in our mother's womb states that while we were being formed that our "days are numbered." Second Timothy 1:9 relates that "God saved us and called us with a holy calling, not according to our works, but according to His own purpose and grace, which was given in Christ Jesus, before the foundation of the earth"? The most profound thought that we can think is how God sees before us. Let's believe that God has purposes that he wants to accomplish through this book. Let's believe that he saw you changing through the reading of this book, before you were born. Wow. Getting excited yet?

Let's consider some of the transgenerational effects of an argumentative spirit. Deuteronomy 30:19-20 relates, "I call heaven and earth to record this day against you, that I have set before you life and death, blessings, and cursing; therefore choose life, that both thou and thy <u>seed may live.</u> That thou mayest love the Lord, thy God, and that thou mayest obey His voice, and thou mayest cleave unto Him; for He is life, and the length of thy days, that thou mayest dwell in the land which the Lord sware unto thy fathers to give thee." Note that the Lord gives both blessings and curses. Note that "blessings and curses" can be transgenerational... both thou and thy seed may live...." In 1 Corinthians 11:29-30 is the warning of taking communion "unworthily." The Scriptures states, "For he that eateth and drinketh unworthily, eateth and drinketh damnation to himself, not discerning the Lord's body. For this cause many are weak and sickly among you, and many sleep." What a thought! Could there possibly be a correlation between a person's sickness and his taking the Lord's Supper "unworthily"? And who is keeping these records? Well, God is, of course. Let's not forget that Galatians 6:7 warns us to "Be not deceived. God is not mocked, for whatsoever a man sows, that shall he also reap. For he that sowsto his flesh shall of the flesh reap corruption, but he that sowsto the Spirit shall of the Spirit reap life everlasting." Grasping this is beyond understanding. God is keeping elaborate records.

The best sermon that I ever heard preached in my life was preached by Dr. Stuart Briscoe. His thoughts were built around God's grace, God's mercy, and God's justice. Praise God, we will take all the grace He wants to give us. Amen. Praise God, we will take all the mercy that He will pour upon us. Amen. Praise God for His justice. We want to get what's coming to us. Amen. Well… wait a minute. But the possible consequences of righteous and unrighteous actions as initiated by God permeate the Scriptures. Think of the possible ramifications to ourselves and to our nation if we would adhere to 2 Chronicles 7:14, "If my people, which are called by my name, shall humble themselves, and pray, and seek my face, and turn from their wicked ways, then will I hear from heaven, and I will forgive their sin, and will heal their land." And all throughout the book of Proverbs we have the contrast between the wise and foolish, and the results of such. Again, who is keeping those records? Proverbs 11:29 states that, "He that troubles his own house shall inherit the wind, and the fool shall be servant to the wise of heart." There are going to be Divine consequences of having an argumentative spirit. I know… I have been there. My wife and children can attest to such.

The main vehicle for "curses and blessings" is words. How many times do we say "God bless you" without considering the ramifications? Proverbs 11:9 states, "The hypocrite with his mouth destroys his neighbors, but through knowledge the just will be delivered." Proverbs 15:4, as we have already quoted, says, "A wholesome tongue is a tree of life, but perverseness therein breaks (crushes) the spirit." Proverbs 18:21 relates that "Death and life are in the power of the tongue, and they that love it will eat the fruit thereof...." Your words not only affect your inner person but potentially can be coded into other family members. That is sobering indeed.

God does indeed "code" us transgenerationally. Exodus 20:5 says, "...for I the Lord thy God am a jealous God, visiting the iniquity of the fathers upon the children unto the third and fourth generation of them that hate me." I believe that I was the product of my grandfather's argumentative spirit. Deuteronomy 28:1ff says "...if thou shalt hearken diligently unto the voice of the Lord thy God... all these blessings shall come on thee... blessed shall be the fruit of thy body... fruit of thy ground... fruit of thy cattle... blessed shalt thy be when thou comest in... and goest out...." This is strongly illustrated through Abraham's sin of deception. In Genesis 12:10-20, he lied about Sarah being his wife. He claimed that she was his sister. And behold, some fourteen chapters following did not Isaac lie about Rebecca being his wife, and he claimed that she was his sister. And this sin of deception was carried down to Isaac's son Jacob (Gen. 27:5-35), and then it went down to Jacob's sons (Gen. 37:12-35). Now folks... this really should get your attention next time you decide to argue with your spouse. Our will is the determiner in part as to whether we are blessed or cursed.

I would suggest the reading of Derek Prince's good book, *Blessing or Curses*, and I would also suggest a thorough study of Deuteronomy 27-28. Dr. Prince suggests five different types of curses:

Mental and Emotional Breakdowns: It is perhaps difficult to imagine a God of grace and mercy that pre-determines "transgenerational" curses. But it must be understood that He is a God of justice. Watch the following passages closely. Deuteronomy 28:28 states, "The Lord shall smite thee with madness [mental], and blindness [spiritually], and astonishment [panic] of heart." Verse 65 says, "...but the Lord shall give thee there a trembling heart, and failing eyes, and sorrow [listlessness] of mind." We can only speculate how many mental and emotional struggles are correlated to curses.

Repeated and Chronic Diseases: Deuteronomy 28:20ff tells us, "The Lord shall send upon thee cursing, vexation and rebuke... the Lord shall make the pestilence cleave unto thee... the Lord shall smite thee with a consumption, and with a fever, and with an inflammation, and with an extreme burning." Could this last one be hemorrhoids? I do believe that we can have "coded tendencies" for certain physical disorders.

Barrenness, a tendency to miscarry or related female problems: It says in Deuteronomy 28:18, "Cursed shall be the fruit of your body... [or of the womb]." This could include the inability to conceive, a tendency to miscarry, failure to menstruate, irregular menstruation, debilitating menstrual cramps, frigidity, cysts, tumors, or some other irregular functions within the reproductive process.

Breakdown of marriage and family alienation—Note how so many family struggles are transgenerational. Deuteronomy 28:41 says, "You shall begat sons and daughter, but they shall not be yours; for they shall go into captivity." There are many other strong prophesies built around the demise of the family. One is Malachi 4:5-6, "…before the coming of the great and dreadful day of the Lord, and he shall turn the hearts of the fathers to the children and the hearts of the children to their fathers, lest I come and strike the earth with a curse." Another is 2 Timothy 3:1-2, "This know also, that in the last days perilous times shall come. For men shall be lovers of their own selves, covetous, boasters, proud, blasphemers, <u>disobedient to parents</u>.…" Let's not forget that the last of the "blessings promised" in Ephesians 6:1-3 is related to our families, "Children obey your parents in the Lord, for this is right. Honor thy father and thy mother, which is the first commandment with promise, <u>that it may be well with thee,</u> and that thou may <u>live long on the earth."</u> If things can be well with me, because I have chosen to give honor to my parents (as the passage states), then God is the source behind this stability and security.

<u>Continuing financial insufficiency</u>: Deuteronomy 28:17,29,47-48, "Cursed shall be your kneading bowl… you shall not prosper in your ways… because you did not serve the Lord your God with joy and gladness of heart, for the abundance of all things, therefore, you shall serve your enemies, whom the Lord will send against you, in hunger, in thirst, in nakedness, and in need of all things…."

In Matthew 12:36-37, we have the solemn warning from Jesus, "But I say unto you that for every idle word that men shall speak, they shall give account of it in the Day of Judgment. For by thy words you shall be justified, and by thy words thou shall be condemned." I am here to confess, the Holy Spirit "pounded" me with this verse. I have let many "idle" words stream from my mouth. Let's take the five symptoms above and listen to ourselves momentarily:

Mental and Emotional disorders: "These kids are driving me crazy. I can't take it anymore."

Repeated or chronic sickness: "Whenever there is a bug around, I seem to catch it...." "Cancer seems to run in the family; I guess I'm next...."

Barrenness, Female Problems: "I don't think I will ever get pregnant."

Breakdown of Marriage and Family: "You never did love me." "Our family can't get together without some type of conflict."

Continual Financial Problems: "I don't know where the money goes." "I can't afford to tithe."

There are various moral and ethical sins that can cause curses. In Deuteronomy 27:15-26, there are twelve moral and ethical sins mentioned, all of which could provoke God's curse. I would suggest that you study these carefully and allow the Holy Spirit to introspect within you. The following is a summary of the main ideas covered in these verses: acknowledging and worshiping false gods, disrespect for parents, all forms of oppression and injustice, especially when directed against the weak and helpless, and all forms of illicit or unnatural sex.

And let's remember that Satan can work through our curses. We have already suggested that Satan's plan is to "steal our joy, kill our spirit, and destroy our souls and body (John 10:10). Ephesians 6:12 makes clear that we "wrestle not against flesh and blood but against principalities and against powers, and against spiritual wickedness in high places." Dearly beloved, let me say the obvious. When we are arguing, when those words are flowing from our mouths, this sets in motion effects beyond our comprehension. We are reinforcing our own sickness; we are allowing Satan to get "footholds" in our lives, and we are affecting our children and grandchildren and great grandchildren.

God does desire to bless us. Malachi 3:10 relates that if we "bring all our tithes into the storehouse, that there will be meat in thine house.... Says the Lord of hosts... I will open for you the windows of heaven and pour out for you such blessings that there will not be room enough to receive it." Praise God He relates that if..." we draw nigh to Him that He will draw nigh to us (James 4:8)," and if we turn to His reproof that He will "pour out His spirit unto us, and will make known His words unto us." Praise the Lord. Will you take all of what He will give to you? And, of course, we have the "beatitudes" in Matthew 5:3-11. He wants us to be "poor in spirit [humble], to be meek, and to be merciful, and to be sympathetic, and to be determined, and be pure, and to be peaceable..." and the results will be that we "will be filled, obtain mercy, inherit the earth, and see God." Getting excited yet?

This material is about to turn from the pessimistic to the optimistic. The last part of this book will deal with the healing process. Let's close this chapter by turning our curses into blessings. James 4:7promises that if we "resist the devil he will flee from us." Such a promise…. But change is dependent on our wills and our volition. We have to have that determination that we are going to conquer our anger and our argumentative spirit. Whenever God wanted to do things differently, He affirmed a New Covenant. Hebrews 10:4ff states, "For by one offering He hath perfected forever them that are sanctified…. This is the <u>covenant</u> that I will make with them after those days, saith the Lord, I will put my laws into their hearts and minds…." Ah folks, how would you like the Lord to put His laws into your hearts and minds? Let me suggest five steps in moving our curses to blessings.

Step One–Realization

Carl Jung was correct when he said, "self realization is the first step of change." In Proverbs 24:32, after presenting the imagery of a "broken down" house, Solomon presents this scenario of change, "Then I saw [realization], and considered it well [reflection], and I looked upon it [identification], and received instruction [change] I would suggest that there are two parts of this first step.

<u>We must identify the curse.</u> Let's take the three passages of Scripture that deal with flesh and lump them together (Gal. 5:19- 21; Mark 7:21-22; and Eph. 5:31). "…bitterness, wrath, anger, clamor [confusion], evil speaking, malice [getting back]… evil thoughts, adulteries, fornications, murders, thefts, covetousness, wickedness, deceit, lasciviousness [lust], evil eye, blasphemy, pride, foolishness… adultery, uncleanness [sexual things], idolatry, witchcraft, hatred, variance [person against person],

emulation's [jealousies], wrath, strife, sedition's, heresies, envying, murders, drunkenness, and revellings…" Now let me give you an exercise. Quickly, find a pen or pencil and circle any of these with which you might struggle. This next statement is very important. Obviously, in the splitting of the human spirit, anger is just one of many attributes of the flesh that can influence and possess our inner person.

We must identify the source. Are there others within your extended family that manifest any of these characteristics? Is it not possible that these struggles of the flesh could have transgenerational origins?

Step Two–Repentance

Repentance is a prerequisite for God's mercy and grace. Let's not forget that awesome passage in Isaiah 53:4-5. "Surely He hath borne our griefs and carried our sorrows; yet we did esteem him stricken, smitten by God and afflicted, but He was wounded for our transgressions, He was bruised for our iniquities, the chastisement of our peace was upon Him; and with His stripes we are healed." You heard it, didn't you? We have the potential to be healed!! Jesus did this for you and for me. I would suggest two steps at this point: (1) We must confess our desire to have this curse and sin removed from us. First John 1:9 says, "If we confess our sins, He is faithful and just to forgive us our sins, and to cleanse us from all unrighteousness." And (2), we must receive the remission [forgiveness] that God has promised. It is not ours until we take it. John 16:23-24 says, "Whatsoever ye shall ask the Father in my name, He will give it you. Hitherto have ye asked nothing in my name. Ask and <u>ye shall receive, that your joy may be full."</u>

Step Three–Release

First Peter 5:7 says, "Casting [releasing] all your care upon Him; for He careth for you." Praise God, the time has come for a releasing of our curses. I would encourage all of us to repeat this prayer (taken from Derek Prince's book):

> "Lord Jesus Christ, I believe that You are the Son of God and the only way to God, and that You died on the cross for my sins and rose again from the dead. I give up all my rebellion and all my sin, and I submit myself to You as my Lord. I confess all my sins before You and ask for Your forgiveness—especially for any sins that exposed me to a curse. Release me from the consequences of my ancestor's sins. By a decision of my will, I forgive all have harmed me or wronged me— just as I want you Father to forgive me. In particular I forgive… [list of people].
>
> "I renounce all contact with anything occult or satanic—if I have any "contact objects (objects that identify with Satan and evil)," I commit myself to destroy them .I cancel all Satan's claims against me. I pray Lord that I may be released from any "footholds" in my body, soul, or spirit that the devil upon me, and in Jesus name… in Jesus name… I pray for release of any evil spirits that might presently control me. Lord Jesus I believe that on the cross You took on

Yourself every curse that could ever come upon me. So I ask You now to release me from every curse over my life—in your name, Lord Jesus Christ. By faith I now receive my release and my blessings. Thank you for peace. Thank you for release in Jesus name."

Step Four–Reconciliation

Many folk know 2 Corinthians 5:17; "Therefore if any man be in Christ, he is a new creature, old things are passed away; behold all things are become new." But the passage continues in verse 18 to relate that IIe has given unto us the "ministry of reconciliation." Later in the passage, Paul relates that He will give unto us the very "words of reconciliation." The word reconciliation literally means, "closing the gap...." It is our job to close the gap with anyone to whom we have been estranged. We first must identify anyone with whom we need to be reconciled. Secondly, we have to cross over into their world. The apostle Paul said that he "became all things to all men, that by some means, he might win some...." It is our task to remake the person in our minds. As Lewis Smedes states in his book *Forgive and Forget*, that "we remake the person in our minds... we should look at them now not as the person who hurt us, but the person who needs us." In interpersonal relationships gaps are not always closed, but we do have the power to remake that person in our minds.

Step Five–Renewal

If you have followed these steps, praise His Holy name, God has renewed you. Romans 12:2 states that we can be "transformed

when Jesus "went into the temple of God, and cast out all them that sold and bought in the temple, and overthrew the tables of the money-changers, and the seats of them that sold doves," was He angry? I think not. You might respond, "Wait a minute. He is turning over tables." He seems to be angry. But we can only conjecture as to what Jesus was feeling. In graduate school I learned about an "objective reaction." This is expressing a strong emotional reaction but being rationally in control. I could assume a certain "persona" when in fact I am very "cool.". There were times with my kids that I would raise my voice and say with great authority, "Clean up that mess right now." Did the kids think I was angry? Yes. Was I? Generally, I was not. This was entirely objective; this was entirely for effect. I think Jesus realized if He had said, "Please guys, pretty please, don't make my Father's house a den of thieves," he would not have had their attention. They got His point. I think He was totally "rational" inwardly.

So let's define anger as an irrational response to a given stimulus. Of course, since we are always rational, this section is not pertinent to us. How about me giving to you a personal confession? My kids are grown, but they have reminded me that one of the "best" arguments between my wife and me occurred in a car traveling from Ann Arbor to Traverse City, Michigan. This is a four and a half-hour trip, and we must have occupied at least two hours of it with harsh words. I was so dumb, and I was so sick. I understand the dynamics now of my irrational behavior.

Basically, we judge others by their words. We have an entire chapter in James 3 dealing with the tongue. Verse 10 relates that "out of the same mouth proceedeth blessing and cursing. My brethren, these things ought not so to be." The passage continues to challenge us that if we are wise and have knowledge, it will be emulated through our "conversation and meekness" (v. 13). Interestingly, both verses 14 and 16 warn us of having "envying and strife" within us. That inner strife affects our tongues.

Matthew 12:36 warns us that ultimately we will be judged by God for our words, "But I say unto you, that every idle word that man shall speak, they shall give account thereof in the Day of Judgment." That is sobering. But Proverbs 25:11 relates that a "word fitly spoken is like apples of gold and pictures of silver." My mother used to have her hair done on Fridays, and inevitably she would return home "fluffing" her hair (she was great), and say, "How do I look?" The next words from my mouth were crucial. "Mom," I would say, "you look _____" (a word fitly spoken…).

This chapter will help us understand "anger" and how it is expressed through argumentation.

We have basically eight emotions. These are love, joy, sorrow, anger, fear, anxiety, jealousy, and hate. Thus, as you recall in our discussion of "Biblical Anthropology" we established that our emotions are located within our soul. In the development of anger there are two variables: (1) development; and (2) capacity. No two individuals have the same capacity for each emotion, and no two individuals have the same environment as to development. As has been discussed because I had a transgenerational curse of anger, it was easier for me to express this. Thus, the amount of anger felt by my wife might differ from the amount of anger felt by me.

Our society promotes the sickness of anger. I was active in athletics both in high school and college. But upon reflection, I am not sure their effects upon me were positive. Consider with me sports like boxing, and wrestling, and soccer, and football. They promote violence. I played some football both in high school and college. When I had a blocking assignment, where my task was to hit a man as hard as I could, did I not reinforce this? Millions of fans vicariously do the same as spectators. How many times have we yelled, "Kill the umpire?" And think of the consequences of violence in video games, movies, and television. Can we imagine a society where all that is removed? Can we imagine a society where we play sports, but we don't keep score? As of this writing, we have soldiers who have been asked to go to war. Are we surprised that they return home and are violent to their spouse or children? I am aware that freedom must be defended, but the toll is paid many times off the battlefield.

What does God want to happen to our emotions? Let's consider three passages.

1 Thessalonians 3:12; "And the Lord make you to <u>increase and abound</u> in love one toward another…." John 15:11, "These things have I spoken unto you that my joy might remain in you, and that <u>your joy might be full.</u>" And finally, Ephesians 4:29-32, "Let no needless communication proceed out of your mouth [get a handle on that thought], but that which is good for the use of edifying, that it may minister grace to the hearers. And grieve not the Holy Spirit of God, whereby ye

are sealed unto the day of redemption. Let all <u>bitterness, and wrath, and anger, and clamor,</u> and evil speaking by put away from you [that's our goal] with all malice. And be ye kind one to another, tenderhearted, forgiving one another, even as God for Christ's sake has forgiven you." It would be good for us to stop and reflect on these passages momentarily.

If arguments are "strong discussions" and anger is a "self-willed" feeling, then both can easily become destructive. During an argument are you open to the other's opinion? Let's suppose for the sake of discussion, that this argument has become "heated" enough that you are now under attack. If your spouse is reminding you how stupid your thinking might be, my guess would be that you are not thinking, "Yes, please tell me more." No you are probably thinking, "As soon as he/she slows down, I am going to remind him/her of their own idiosyncrasies."

The premise of an argument is simple. I believe that if I talk long enough, or loud enough, or logical enough (note three l's), I will persuade my opponent to change his/her mind. Now come on. It took me years to understand that when I am arguing with my wife, I am forcing her to defend an issue that I believe to be wrong. It becomes counter-productive because she is reinforcing her beliefs with every word. Thus, we have the insight as to why people argue more than once over the same issue. And tragically, sometimes, this continues for years. Provocative... huh? Sick people argue. Healthy people can be quiet. Let's remember... Proverbs 17:27 says, "He that hath knowledge spares his words; and a man of understanding is of an excellent (cool) spirit." As previously stated... my goal

He had his bags packed and He was going home to mother (which he did). In the other situation, the husband had been unfaithful to his wife. When I arrived, he was in the yard, and we chatted for awhile. He gave permission for me to go into the house. As I entered the house, a plate came flying over my head. The wife was so angry with her husband that she was ready to hit him with a plate when he walked through the door. Fortunately, for me she was both a poor shot and a very apologetic person.

An argument augmented with anger can escalate to rage, resentment, and indignation. Rage is violent and explosive and manifested outwardly. Resentment is rage turned inside. It is repressed feelings of anger that usually smolder and seek revenge. Indignation is controlled feelings of justice. Note that indignation has a rational basis. From his excellent book, *Anger, Yours and Mine and What to Do About It,* Richard Walters makes these comparisons:

1. Rage seeks to do wrong. Resentment seeks to hide wrong. Indignation seeks to correct wrongs.
2. Rage and resentment seek to destroy people. Indignation seeks to destroy evil.
3. Rage and resentment seek vengeance. Indignation seeks justice.
4. Rage is guided by selfishness. Resentment is guided by cowardice. Indignation is guided by mercy.
5. Rage uses open warfare. Resentment is a guerilla fighter. Indignation is a honest, fearless, forceful, defender of truth.

6. Rage defends itself. Resentment defends the status quo. Indignation defends the other person.
7. Rage and resentment are forbidden in the Bible. Indignation is encouraged.

There are basically three Greek words for anger in the New Testament. Each one expresses a different nuance of anger.

(1) Anger is defined by *tumos*. This is a turbulent, boiling, agitation of feelings. It blazes up like a sudden explosion, and then it quickly subsides. We get our word tumult from this word. It is much like a match that blazes quickly and then subsides. It is mentioned some twenty times in the New Testament. Many times it is translated with the word "wrath." Ephesians 4:31 says, "Let all bitterness, and wrath [tumos], and anger... be put away from you." Galatians 5:19-20, "Now the works of the flesh are manifest which are these: adultery, fornication, uncleanness, lasciviousness, idolatry, witchcraft, hatred, variance, emulation, wrath [tumos], and strife...." Obviously, a person with a wounded or crushed individual, who has become ill-tempered, can easily develop an argumentative spirit. Because their spirit is fractured, it is easy for them to "go off the handle" and to express themselves through strife and wrath. Proverbs 17:1 states, "Better is a dry morsel and quietness therewith, than a house full of sacrifices and strife." You can serve steak dinners, but if there is wrath in your home, you will never have a healthy family.

(2) Anger is defined by *orgay*. This word has the connotation of a settled, long lasting attitude. The person internalizes the anger. They are usually reflective and bent upon hurting

back. "Orgay" could be likened to coals slowly warming up to red, then to white, and staying hot while holding a high temperature. This word is in the New Testament some forty-five times. It is translated both anger and wrath. Ephesians 4:31 states, "Let all bitterness, and wrath, and anger [orgay]… be put away from you." Romans 12:19-20 says, "Dearly beloved, avenge not yourselves, nor give place unto wrath [orgay], for it is written, Vengeance is mine. I will repay saith the Lord. Therefore if thine enemy hunger, feed him: if he is thirsty, give him drink. For in so doing thou shalt heap coals of fire of fire on his head." I call people with an orgay type of anger "scorekeepers." They are thinking, "You think I don't know what is happening, but I do. Someday, you will want something from me, and the answer is already no." Within marriage many times money and sex become weapons. Tumos people are reactionary individuals; the orgy people are more reflective. Let's imagine tension between a reactionary and a reflective person.

(3) <u>Anger is also defined by *parorgismos*</u>. This is an anger that has been provoked. It is used three times in the New Testament. Ephesians 6:4, "Fathers provoke [parorgismos] not your children to wrath [parorgismos], but nurture them in the fear and admonition of the Lord." The interchange here is interesting. If I have an attitude of strife, and I express this adamantly to my children, I should not be surprised if they also express anger and wrath accordingly. In my Marriage and Family Class at William Tyndale College, I ask the students, "Were you ever slapped in the face?" Many of them can not only relive the circumstances, but they can tell me on what

day of the week it happened. They were provoked. They perhaps deserved discipline, but they did not deserve to be slapped in the face. In all candor, this expression of anger is the most difficult for me. If I am "minding my own business" and someone wants to provoke me, I have to be careful not to respond accordingly. After a recent conference, I started home only to have a "young buck" come up against my bumper. The speed limit was 50 MPH on a two-lane highway. I was going 50, but he wanted to go 90. The sick part of me said, "Well, if you don't like 50, let's try 40." I had been provoked. The healthy side of me said, "Pull over and let him pass." Which I did. As I was parked along the highway, I thought, "Twenty years ago the outcome would have been much different." Thank you Father for your grace and mercy. I believe someone right now needs this.

We are now ready to move toward the healing of the argumentative spirit.

CHAPTER EIGHT

HEALING THE ARGUMENTATIVE SPIRIT–
The Process

These next three chapters, if applied, could not only stop all domestic problems, but this material applied could impact international problems. Eventually, our prisons could be emptied. You can judge the veracity of this claim. I do believe that applying these three chapters is an imperative for healing.

According to the Bible, there are two ways that people can change. They can change through "renewal" and through "restoration." David, in pleading before the Lord in Psalm 51 after his sin with Bathsheba, cried, "Create in me a clean heart, O God; and renew a right spirit within me. Cast me not away from thy presence; and take not thy Holy Spirit from me." David came before the Lord with a repentant heart. If only that would be our starting point. If only we would desire to rid ourselves of any sins, I believe that God would honor that spirit. Who has been hurt through your argumentative spirit? After you come before the Lord, I would suggest that you make a list of individuals to whom you need to apologize. Note that David was concerned about the Lord taking his Holy Spirit from him. In Romans 1:29, God gives individuals over to a "reprobate mind." Our stubbornness and lack of contrition keeps us from knowing the blessings of God in our lives. Note, also, that David desired to be "renewed." "Renew a right spirit within me." This word "renew" is mentioned throughout Scripture. In Isaiah 40:31, those that "wait upon the Lord" can have their strength renewed. Romans 12:2, "challenges us to not be conformed to this world, but be ye transformed by the renewing of your mind...."

The Greek and Hebrew words for "renew" connote thoughts like "rebuilding" or "renovating." I like the thought set forth in one of the commentaries of being "better than new." How would you like to drive your car for 200,000 miles, and then one-day walk outside and find that it has been renewed? The car is better than new. Praise God, it is not where we have been, it is where we are going. Brace yourself for a real renewal.

Obviously however, if we are sick from erethism, and if we have a fractured spirit, we initially need a healing within our spirits. It is intriguing that since anger is one of our emotions, and in this culture the "heart" was considered the "emotional center" of the individual, that David's request was for a real cleansing of his emotions. Among the possible translations of the word "right" in our passage (right spirit), is the word "perfect" or "correct." God desires to renew us. God is striving to draw from us holiness, righteousness, and perfection (Matt. 5:48; Eph. 4:24). Are you getting excited yet?

Imagine with me a new society. In this society we have not only clinics for the healing of physical and mental disorders; we have clinics for the healing of emotional disorders. Many years ago, I began counseling a young man who was eventually incarcerated on a second-degree murder charge. He became angry over "homosexual advances" by an older man, and he bludgeoned this man to death with a knife and a rifle barrel. I committed myself to visiting him during his imprisonment. In one of my first sessions, I made an appointment to visit his counselor. After some discussion concerning my counseling of him, I inquired how he would be helping him. His remarks are fixed in my mind; "Do you think I am a counselor? I am a paper pusher. I am responsible for 168 men. I don't have time to personally counsel them individually." Our society is so prone to deal with the effect and not the cause. In the society that I envision, when any anger or rage is manifested, the individual and family must get emotional help. Among the purposes of the emotional healing clinics would be a "renewal" of their spirits. The purpose in part of these clinics would be to totally "rebuild" and "renovate" the very "essence of life" within the individual, within his spirit.

We have dissipated so much. Would it not be better to "rebuild" the lives of our prison inmates? We must not only renew our spirit; we must also restore our souls. Let's remember that the soul is the interpretive part of our personality. David in Psalm 51 asks of God to "restore unto me the joy of thy salvation...." The 23rd Psalm begins, "The

Lord is my shepherd; I shall not want. He maketh me to lie down in green pastures; he leadeth me beside the still waters, He restoreth my soul." The Hebrew word for restore is *sheva* meaning a returning to the starting point. I sometimes ask couples during counseling, "When was the happiest time in your marriage?" Now for the healthy couple, the correct answer should be today. But many of the couples struggle to recall a happier time. Psalm 23 implies that all of us are in a state of flux. There is no "status quo." You are either happier or sadder today than you were yesterday. You are either more or less spiritual today than you were yesterday. And yes, you are either more or less angry today than you were yesterday. Probably, in a war setting, anger will escalate to rage. The escalation will continue until the conscience is seared and a man will be able to kill with no feelings of remorse. Just this day, I heard on the radio that Palestinian soldiers arrested a Palestinian woman. She was accused of abetting the enemy. They took her to another building and shot her. My guess would be that the Palestinian soldier did not lose any sleep that night. Think of Timothy McVee who bombed the Federal Building in Oklahoma City. He probably believed, right to his death, that he was right and everyone else was wrong. I would surmise that he gave little thought to the many innocent lives that were lost.

Before we walk through the steps of healing, let's consider that triggering mechanism within the spirit. It takes little for the triggering to occur. "Honey, would you take out the garbage?" That seems an innocent enough request. But I can think of a couple that I counseled for whom the taking out of the garbage became the battlefield. She wanted him to daily do this. He resisted. She would leave the bag by the back door. He resisted. She would leave it on the walk to the car. He would walk by it. Finally, one night when he came home late, he noticed that the garbage was gone. He assumed that he had won, but that night when he got into his twin bed, he discovered that it was filled with garbage. Something very small had become very large.

What do you feel when you are belittled? What do you feel when your spouse verbally attacks you? Again, understanding that triggering mechanism is very important.

(1) <u>There is an ignition.</u> Ecclesiastes 7:9 states, "Be not hasty in thy spirit to be angry; for anger resteth in the bosom of fools." The Hebrew word for "hasty" means to "tremble inwardly, or to be agitated." The first thing that I must understand about this "triggering mechanism" is that it only takes a spark to ignite it. I must become conscious of that potential spark. To me, the strongest integration passage in the Scriptures is the Sermon on the Mount. When thinking of this "triggering mechanism," imagine the response to the teachings of Jesus when he said "agree with thine adversary quickly...? (Matt. 5:25). If someone "smites thee on thy right cheek, turn to him the other also." (5:39) Are you observing that Jesus is promoting an entirely new system of conflict resolution? ..." . "

Obviously, we all deal with tensions differently. Here a few options:

There is the <u>denier.</u> This person <u>represses</u> the anger. He chooses to deal with tensions by not dealing with them. This is the non-confrontational person. He is generally reflective and internalizes his tensions.

There is the <u>stuffer</u>. This person <u>suppresses</u> the anger. He does personalize it, but he also holds it in. This is the "orgay" anger. He becomes a scorekeeper. He will look for opportunities for revenge.

There is the <u>yeller</u>. This person <u>expresses</u> the anger. This is the "tumos" or "parorgismos" anger. This is the "scoffer" in Proverbs 9. This is the individual who must have the last word. Imagine if both the husband and wife were yellers; it generally takes little to ignite the spirit.

There is the <u>processor.</u> This person <u>confesses</u> the anger. The goal of these last chapters is to make processors from deniers, stuffers, and yellers. Getting excited yet? To become a processor you must move from the emotional to the rational. You must move from the emotional to the volitional.

(2) <u>There is volition</u>. (will modification) James 4:1-5 states, "From whence come wars and fightings among you? Come they not hence, even of your lusts that war in your members. Ye lust, and have not; ye kill, and desire to have, and cannot obtain; ye fight and war, yet ye have not... the spirit that dwelleth in us lusteth to envy." Wars are not fought over land or philosophy, they are fought over pride and greed. Our proof text in Proverbs 16:32 states, "he that is slow to anger is better than the mighty, and he that rules his spirit can take a city." How do you rule your spirit? It is not easy. At the moment of the stimulus, during the ignition phase, I must decide by volition that my response will not be one of anger. I will not argue. I believe that the greatest psychological passage

the person in bondage to an argumentative spirit. Our conscience can be "seared" and there is little guilt for all the massive arguments. We certainly would not say I'm sorry, to our spouse or to God. God is striving to move us from law to grace. Let Romans 8:2 ring in our ears, "For the law of the Spirit of life in Christ Jesus hath made me free [that's free] from the law of sin and death." God wants to free us from ourselves and move us to grace. Let me illustrate. When I was a young man, my wife told me I had a bit of a "heavy foot" while driving. There was a time or two that the "law" reminded me that she was correct. Now that I am much older, I drive the Detroit freeways to get to the college. The speed limit is 70 miles per hour, and I am generally under that on the inside lane. My point is that they can post any speed limit they want. I have moved from "law to grace." I drive the speed limit now not because I have to but because I want to. It is amazing isn't it? My point is that as you progress through sanctification, you will discover a complete metamorphosis in your argumentative spirit. You will say within yourself, "I can't believe that in the past this type of statement would have 'duped' me into an argument." When you have the realization during this triggering phase, you are moving from law to grace.

(3) <u>God wants to move us from contention to meekness and humility.</u> God's goals for argumentative people are meekness and humility. I said, "God's goal for argumentative people is meekness and humility." Let me shout it, "GOD'S GOAL FOR ARGUMENTATIVE PEOPLE IS MEEKNESS AND HUMILITY."

I like to define humility as "understanding who we are in relationship to whom God is." Imagine how our space program is viewed from God's perspective. Assume for a moment that God is the creator of the universe. He put the sun and stars in place. And then one day, He observes this small "metal can" [rocket ship] headed for one of His created moons. The universe magnifies God. The rocket ship shrinks man. It makes little difference how many years you have been to college or how many books you have read, compared to God we "know nothing about nothing." But it is more than this. Just beginning to understand this Awesome God should drive us to our knees in meekness and humility. Compared to God, we should be lowly and contrite. James 4:10 states that if we "humble ourselves in the sight of the Lord that He will lift us up." The opposite of humility is pride. It has been said that the reason God is hard on prideful people is because "pride is taking on God-like qualities." We think that we are all knowing, etc.… James 4:6 relates that "God resisteth the proud and giveth grace to the humble." Proverbs 22:4 says that "by humility and fear of the Lord are riches, and honor, and life." How would you like to have riches and honor and life? Well your task is easy, you just have to become humble and develop an awesome reverence for God.

The first step of healing is having a desire to move our attitude from contention to humility and meekness.

Meekness has been described as "quiet power"… I know that I am right; so why get excited. But it is stronger than that. The original word means "mild." How much would we have to change to become mild? Meekness not anger is triggered during stress. We have moved from being "high strung" to easygoing. I had a "father-in-law" that was indeed a meek man. I don't recall ever seeing him express anger. He never got into an argument. He would state his opinion and he was done. Do we understand the strength of Jesus' words in Matthew 11:28-30, "Come unto me all ye that labor and are heavy laden, and I will give you rest. Take my yoke upon you and learn of me, for I am meek and lowly in heart, and ye shall find rest unto your souls. For my yoke is easy, and my burden is light." God desires for us to have rest in our souls. God desires us to become mild. The strongest passage that correlates this anti-thesis between contention and meekness is James 3:13-l7. Hold onto something. This is a dynamic truth. "Who is a wise man and endued with knowledge among you? Let him shew out of a good conversation his works with meekness of wisdom (that's meekness of wisdom). But if ye have bitter envying and strife in your hearts, glory not, and lie not against the truth. This wisdom descendeth not from above, but is earthly, sensual, devilish (that's devilish). For where there is envying and strife there is confusion (disorder) and every evil work. But the wisdom that is from above is first pure, then peaceable, gentle, and easy to be intreated, full of mercy and good fruits, without partiality, and without hypocrisy...." Do you sense the "sanctifying" process? Do you sense a righteous God, through the Holy Spirit, desiring to make some dynamic changes within you?

We are ready to dissect the structure for change. Hold on.

CHAPTER NINE

HEALING THE ARGUMENTATIVE SPIRIT—
The Structure

Who corrects you? To whom do you go for counsel? Obviously, this chapter is crucial in our changing from contention to meekness, from being prideful to being humble. During an argument, when someone is attempting to change your mind, are you listening for correction or are you thinking rebuttal. This chapter will focus on correction. Let's suggest that your willingness to be corrected is a decisive key in the healing of an argumentative spirit. Bill Gothard speaks to this in his levels of friendship. He has four levels: acquaintance, casual, close, and intimate.

Here are his definitions. An acquaintance he defines as the freedom to know someone on a name to name basis. How many people know that you are alive, and when they see you they know you by name? Think of a number and write it down. The second level is the casual friend. Casual friendship is the freedom to have something in common with someone else. This would include people at work, school, church, etc. Again, write down that number. The third level is the close friend. With how many people in this vast world do you have the freedom to share your ideas, thoughts and feelings? With how many people in this vast world do you share your ideas and thoughts? Again write down a number. The last level is what Bill Gothard calls an intimate friend. This is someone who has the freedom to correct you, and you have the freedom to correct him or her. How many people do you know of this level? Write down that number. Is not this declination amazing? A greatly ignored passage is James 5:16, "Confess your faults one to another, and pray one for another, that ye may be healed…." When was the last time you attended a service at your church where people were "confessing their faults one to another?" I have lived a few years, and I have never attended such a service. The key to changing your argumentative spirit is a willingness to be corrected.

Let's go one step deeper. Proverbs 9:6-10 states, "Forsake the foolish, and live; and go in the way of understanding. He that reproves a scorner gets to himself shame and he that rebukes a wicked man gets himself a blot. Reprove not a scorner, lest he hate thee, rebuke a wise man, and he will love thee. Give instruction to a wise man, and he will be yet wiser, teach a just man, and he will increase in learning. The fear of the Lord is the beginning of wisdom, and the knowledge of the holy is understanding." Please note the movement in verse six. We are moving from foolishness to life, and we are getting on the "way of understanding." How would like to get on the path of understanding?

You will also note that there are three different people in the passage: (1) the wicked man, or the fighter; (2) the scorner, or the teller; and (3) the wise man, or the listener.

Let's ask ourselves, which one of these best characterizes us? Note that if you try to correct the wicked man, you will get a blot. This is a physical blemish. Why do people fight, or hit, or abuse others? Are they not striving to force their will on others? If you try to correct a scorner, he will attempt to shame you. A scorner will hate you. That's strong language. The word "scorner" literally in Hebrew means, "one who makes with the mouth." This person has an opinion about everything. You can bring up any topic that you desire, and they will tell you where you are wrong. The scorner always wants to have the last word. Finally, there is the wise man. "Rebuke a wise man, and he will love you...." This is the person we want to become. Are you getting excited yet? How much would you have to change to become open to correction? As a wise person, you will want others to correct you? Right? You are open to others opinions.

I was studying this passage for a radio broadcast, when the Holy Spirit profoundly illuminated me. He said to me, "Duane, you are a scorner. In your teaching and counseling, you are giving answers continually, but who corrects you? You desire wisdom, but you are not willing to be corrected?" I was hit. That night when I went home, I said to my wife, "Honey, I want you to correct me." Well, after she hit the floor, and the shock subsided, she said, "You can't be serious." I related that I was very, very serious, and I shared how the Holy Spirit had convicted me. I promised that I would offer no rebuttal. Well, she began… and she talked… and she talked. I thanked her, and then I went to two friends. Neither of them were "professional" people, but they were older, and they knew me well. After they realized that I was serious, they offered correction. I related to one man, "If you had been thinking these thoughts all of these years, why didn't you share them?" He related that you just don't go to others and say, "I think you would be a better person if you would change the following qualities." I can relate that this experience was "life changing" for me. Well now, are you ready to change? Are you ready to be corrected?

There are four steps in changing:

(1) The Rational Phase–Do I understand the need for change? All changes must start on a rational base.
(2) The Revelation Phase–What biblical principles have been violated?
(3) The Reinforcement Phase–How do I inculcate these principles into my life?
(4) The Rebuilding Phase–How do I get these truths into my mind and emotions?

We will attempt to apply these steps in removing our argumentative spirit, but obviously they can be applied to any other of our struggles.

(l) <u>The Rational Phase</u>—Everyone has his or her own way of thinking. Let's speculate as to how differences in ideas are developed. As of this writing I have been married for fifty-three years. I recall during the first year of our marriage, we "quarreled" over the toilet paper. I came from a home where the toilet paper was rolled under (the only correct way) and she came from a home where the toilet paper was rolled over (can you imagine?). When we visited the bathroom, we would turn the paper back and forth. Ridiculous, isn't it? Now, how many of you know of "equally dumb" tensions that were in your marriage?

In the Personality Theory class at the college where I teach, I ask the students to name their favorite candy bar or their favorite color. Then I will challenge them, "How did that get to be your favorite color or candy bar?" Few have an explanation. All of us have thousands of these "constructs." A construct is a set pattern of thinking. We have thousands built within us.

Let's explore again our proof text in Proverbs 16:32, "He that is slow to anger is better than the mighty, and he that rules his spirit than he that takes a city." Most argumentative people are neither "slow to anger" nor do they "rule" their spirit. In this rational phase, we must become aware of the potential of triggering anger and argumentation. This is difficult but imperative. Let's consider two other Scriptures. Proverbs 16:14 states, "The wrath of a king is as messengers of death, but a wise man will pacify it." Do you irritate or do you pacify? The word pacify means to subdue. Again note the "rational consciousness." Your intent is not to make things worse but to make them better. Proverbs 19:11 says, "The discretion of a man defers his anger, and it is his glory to pass over a transgression." The word "discretion" connotes understanding. He does not have to be drawn into argument. He understands. The word "defer" means to "draw out" or "to lengthen." He lengthens his response time. He is not one who immediately responds. Most people with argumentative spirits have quick opinions and quick retorts.

Let's raise a few "rhetorical" questions:

> Do you want to change?
> Do you understand that you have a problem?
> Do you understand how my problems have affected others? Are you willing to accept a new pattern (a new construct) of thinking?

(2) The Revelation Phase Let's review. We have now moved into "rational consciousness," and we are willing to be rebuilt by biblical principles? In marriage counseling I relate, "There are four viewpoints in this room, your two viewpoints, my viewpoint, and His viewpoint (I point to the Bible). Only one of them is totally correct. Are you willing to follow His viewpoint? Are you willing to move from the maladaptive to the adaptive?

We have mentioned 2 Peter 1:4, "Whereby are given to us exceeding great and precious promises that we might be partakers of His Divine nature, having escaped the corruption that is in the world through lust." How would you like to become a partaker of His Divine nature? What a promise. God utilizes His Word to move us toward perfection, holiness, righteousness, and sanctification. We get there by inculcating biblical principles (great and precious promises) into our lives. I contend that for any psychological and spiritual struggle there is a biblical solution. Getting excited yet?

We will cover this in the next chapter, but let's take one principle to stimulate your interest. James 1:19-20 states, "Wherefore, my beloved brethren, let every man be <u>swift to hear, slow to speak, slow to wrath: For the wrath of man worketh not the righteousness of God."</u> This "wrath of man" is *orgay* our scorekeeper. This is the person who manifests his or her rage. If you want to work against the will of God, be wrathful. The admonition is that we should be "slow to speak, slow to wrath [same word], and swift to hear." It hit me that we turn the admonitions in this verse around. Many of us are slow to hear, swift to speak, and swift to wrath. It has been said that God gave to us two ears and one mouth; so we could listen twice as much as we talk. Many of us need to work on that principle.

Some rhetorical questions:

> Do I understand my maladaptive instincts?
> Am I ready to become renewed?
> Am I willing to conform to biblical principles?

(3) <u>The Reinforcement Phase</u> How do we rebuild our constructs? How do we inculcate Biblical principles into our minds? One of my academic heroes was Paul Tournier. In his book *Understanding Ourselves* he related that if we act how we want to feel, we will feel what we want to become (paraphrase). When I read that I leaped. To me it "screamed" truth, truth, and truth. When I was younger I coined the phrase that "any of us can be a hypocrite until finally it becomes us." This was my way of saying that you are to set your goals mentally and give your emotions time to catch up. Eventually, these thoughts by Paul Tournier became known as the "fake it until you feel it syndrome." Many disagreed with the concept. But for me it became the carrier for change. Whatever the biblical principle, it must be lived, practiced, and reinforced, until finally the changes begin.

Let's review. My spirit was wounded and I became sick. It affected my "interpretative" processes. At times I was bitter and enraged. It carried over into my interpersonal relationships. The devil established a "foothold" in my life. It became transgenerational to my children. But praise the Lord, I am now rationally choosing to change. I am willing to conform to biblical principles. I now know how to become this different person. I am going to take principles on anger and argumentation from God's word, and I am "going to fake it until I feel it." I am aware that initially I might not notice much change, but by keeping the "promises" (principles) constantly before me, it will eventually change my soul and spirit.

When I was a young man, I played basketball. I heard that "if you can shoot a jump shot, there will always be a place for you on the basketball team." Now what is being said is that the goal of the game of basketball is to score points. I would like to bear witness that this is true. I use to practice shooting jump shots by the hour. A hero of mine became Johnny Paxton of the Chicago Bulls professional basketball team. Emblazoned in my mind are closing seconds of one of the Bulls championship games. They were down by two points, and they called a time out. Everyone assumed that they would build a play around Michael Jordan, but no they decided to call on "my man" Johnny Paxton. He was known for his ability to shoot jump shots. They set a screen for him, and he released a three-point shot. He hit it and won the game. Can we speculate how many times he had practiced that shot? He, not Michael Jordan, was my hero. Do you want to change? It is easy. All you have to do is practice, practice, and practice.

Many years ago, after a conference, a beautiful, elderly lady corrected me. During the session, I had made the statement that "practice makes perfect." She kindly corrected me. She related, "In due respect Dr. Cuthbertson, practice does not make perfect, <u>practicing perfection makes perfect.</u>" Wow!!! Was she right? With our argumentative spirit, many of us have practiced imperfection for years. Now the challenge is to conform our thinking to biblical principle and practice perfection, practice perfection, practice perfection...Jesus concluded His awesome teachings in the Sermon the Mount (Matt. 5-7) by saying,

"… everyone who hears these words of mine and <u>puts them into practice</u> is like a wise man who built his house on the rock. The rain came down, the streams rose, and the winds blew and beat against that house; yet it did not fall…." Did you hear it? All we have to do is "put these principles into practice." No problem….

Some rhetorical questions:

> Can you identify the imperfections that you've been practicing?
>
> Are you willing to begin applying biblical principles to your life?
>
> Are you willing to practice them?

(4) <u>The Rebuilding Phase</u> Remember change does not occur until our feelings change. We think with our hearts. We are ultimately governed by our emotions. Proverbs 23:7 states, "For as he thinketh in his heart, so is he…." John 14:21 is a favorite passage of mine: "He that hath my commandments, and keepeth them, he it is that loveth me; and he that loveth me shall be loved of my Father, and I will love him, and will manifest myself to him." How would you like to be loved by God and to have Him manifest Himself to you? Amen. Note the correlation of our love for God and the keeping of His commandments. Our feelings ultimately must be changed. So to alleviate an argumentative spirit, it must begin with the rational; it challenges us to conform to Biblical principles on the topic; it stimulates us to reinforce these principles into our lives, until finally it changes our feelings. Easy huh?

I created this illustration comparing the regular and the Biblical Emotional Cycles.

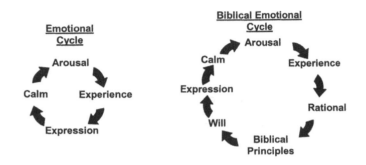

Our regular cycle starts with arousal. It goes to experience, then to expression and to calm. Let's apply this to argumentation. Something is said that arouses us. This experience leads to an expression. Perhaps we argue into the night. Finally, perhaps hours later, there is finally calm.

Now, let's apply biblical theory to this cycle. Note that after the arousal and experience, we move into a rational grid. We become determined to let our minds lead us and not our emotions. After we have activated the rational, we are now ready to apply biblical principles to this arousal. What does the Bible say about this? Of course, this concept not only applies to an argumentative spirit but it applies to lust, depression, guilt, etc. Please note that the next step in the biblical cycle is will. We have a sin nature. As stated in past chapters we have sin, and flesh, and the world, and the devil working against us. So this structure has little value, unless you are motivated and determined to commit yourself to change. Now finally, within this cycle, you are ready for expression and calm.

God desires so much for us emotionally. He expresses these desires through Biblical principles. Think with me. How would you like to be able to "rejoice in the Lord always?" (Phil. 4:4) How would you like to have a joy that's "full?" (John 15:11) How you like to have a love that "abounds?" (Phil. 1:9; 1 Thess. 3:12) How would like to "rule your spirit?" (Prov. 16:32) Praise God. Praise God.

CHAPTER TEN

HEALING THE ARGUMENTATIVE SPIRIT—
The Changed Person

Well it has been an interesting journey. We have introduced you to "Biblical Anthropology" and walked with you through the structure of a person. We specifically analyzed the spirit and soul. We defended that "people who argue are sick," showing that for argumentative people, as a result of being wounded or crushed, their spirits can become fractured (erethism). For some, especially those who have "inherited a maladaptive tendency to respond to argumentation," this can develop an interpretive soul of rage and bitterness. Tragically, Satan can utilize this to get a "foothold" in our lives.

Our desire is to be healed, and we know that God can renew us and move us from contention to meekness, from pride to humility. He desires for us to conform ourselves to biblical principles and for our "heart" (emotions) to be changed. Remember our key verse Proverbs 17:27 states, "He that hath knowledge spares his words and a man of understanding is of an <u>excellent (cool)</u> spirit." The principle here is one of self-control. God wants us to be "cool" in the face of tension. It doesn't quite follow teen vernacular, but it does imply that when others are upset, there is at least one person who is "refined and cool." As a result of our study, there are least four areas where we are challenged to change.

<u>Change Number One: Your understanding has been opened.</u> Let's define understanding as the "process of gaining insight." Some call this process illumination, revelation, or self-realization. In Luke 24, the resurrected Jesus confronted his disciples. They were not aware that it was Jesus. The passage relates in verse 27 that He opened to them first the Scriptures. We have attempted to do that in this material. Secondly, in verse 31, the passage relates that "their eyes were opened and they knew him...." Hopefully; your eyes have been opened concerning your argumentative spirit. Verse 32 is so insightful; it relates that "they said one to another, did not our heart burn within us...." As you anticipate this "new you" that God is building, are you excited? Is your heart burning within you? Then, finally, in verse 45 He "opened their understanding." Do you understand and see it differently?

I recall a lady whose four-year-old son picked up her husband's service revolver (he was a policemen) and, in what he thought to be play, pointed the gun toward his two-year-old brother. The trigger was pulled, a bullet was discharged, and the child was killed instantly. She ran to the scene, picked up the child, and in total hysteria rushed from neighbor to neighbor screaming for help. The child had been killed instantly, but she had no defenses to accept it. The event triggered a delusion, and not only was their denial concerning the death of Danny, but also she was compulsively driven to find the "anti-Christ." She would not allow us to admit her willingly into a hospital, because the admitting psychiatrist could not pass her "religious examination." My first three counseling sessions with this lady were Bible studies on eschatology (doctrine of end times). She would bring reams of notes and stacks of books to our sessions. She would talk incessantly. She came to the fourth session subdued. There were no notes or books. I looked at her said; "Danny is dead, isn't he?"

She looked up somewhat puzzled and responded, "Yes, Danny is dead." She then cried hysterically. The crying must have continued for two minutes. I held her and the tears flowed onto my shirt. At this point the actual therapy was initiated.

Author and Christian statesmen Watchmen Nee refers to this process as intuition. He believes that intuition is the sensing organ of the spirit. His defense of the idea includes verses such as Mark 2:8, where Jesus, "...perceived in his spirit...." The thought is a bit fascinating. Is it not? The notion of a sensing process within the human spirit has many ramifications. In his book, *The Spiritual Man* Watchmen Nee says, "It is through the intuition part of the spirit that we are able to distinguish what is from God and what is not... there is only one kind of truth that is valuable concerning God and that is the truth that is revealed in our spirit by God's Spirit." We sense the need for change, and intuition is used of God to initiate this process.

When we can move along this process of intuition to what we have defined as rational consciousness, we have the potential to experience understanding. We can understand our argumentative spirit.

<u>Change Number Two: Your communication skills can change</u>. Before us now is the challenge of conforming our spirit and soul to biblical principles. How should our journey thus far change our communication skills? If our argumentative spirit has been healed, how are we different? Let's consider four possibilities. Now understand, there are many more.

(1) <u>Learn to say it and be quiet.</u> Matthew 5:37 states, "Let your communication be yes, yes, and no, no, and whatsoever is more than this comes from the evil one." Note the words "from the evil one." The implication is that if our self-control is so limited that we cannot express our opinions and be quiet, the devil is listening and he will become the instigator behind the continuous words. I recall hearing a lady discipline her children with the question, "What part of no do you not understand?" She had made clear to her child that he was not getting his way, and she was closing the discussion. I must confess that it was never easy for me to walk away from an argument. I had to have the last word… and the last word… and the last word. I love the passage in Proverbs 16:23 which states, "The heart of the wise teacheth his mouth and addeth learning to his lips." It is interesting how the heart "teaches" the mouth. Now there is a concept.

(2) <u>Learn how to respond softly.</u> Proverbs 15:1 says, "A soft answer turneth away wrath; but grievous words stir up anger." The word for "grievous" is "pointed and sharp." The word for soft is "weak or faint." How much would we have to change to move from saying words that are sharp and hurtful to words that are weak and faint? While directing a Christian radio station, I received a call from an irate advertiser. My secretary forewarned me, "This person is mad." She was correct. Even though I directed a Christian station, obviously, all of our advertisers were not religious people. When I lifted the phone, he began, "Let me tell you…" and in no uncertain terms he did…. Frankly, some of his points were exaggerated, but some points were well taken. His comments were sharp and grievous. It is amazing what biblical principle can do. My wounded spirit felt the need to retort and my "hurting" soul said to present a rebuttal, but the Lord was laying the foundation, even then for these words that you are reading. Believe it or not… as he was talking I thought of these biblical principles. "He must eventually stop," I pondered. When he stopped, the first thing from my mouth was, "I am sorry, will you forgive us? Tell me please what I can do to make it right." Immediately, the tone of his voice went down, and we were able to amicably work through a resolution. This principle can change the tone of your voice.

(3) <u>Learn to edify others with your words.</u> There are two strong passages to share at this point. Romans 15:1-2 states, "We then that are strong ought to bear the infirmities of the weak, and not to please ourselves. Let every one of us please his neighbor for his good to edification." Ephesians 4:29 states,

of the outer man." I call it the modification of the will. Why have you had the particular circumstances of your life? Why has your life had so much stress and tension? Is it possible that you have "misread" God's purpose in all of this? Watchmen Nee suggested that there must be an "annihilation" of the soul and body. The understanding of these next thoughts is crucial. It is clear from Scripture that God must take us through stress and crises to change us. (Heb. 12) If we do not perceive this "will modification" process is from God, we become selfish, and we become vulnerable to the splitting and fracturing of the spirit. Watchmen Nee is suggesting that there must be a breaking of the outer man for proper filling of the inner man. Man tragically many times is incapable of understanding and perceiving the dynamics of God's purposes behind our struggles. From his book, *The Release of the Spirit,* Nee relates,

> "Our spirit is given to us by God to enable us to respond to Him. But the outward man is ever responding to things without, hence depriving us from the presence of God. We cannot destroy all the things without, but we can break down the outward man... If, through the mercy of God, our outward man is broken, we may be characterized as the following: yesterday, we were full of curiosity, but today it is impossible to be curious. Formerly, our emotions could be easily aroused, either stirring our love, the most delicate emotion or provoking our temper, the crudest of them. But no matter how many thing crowd upon us, now our inward man

remains unmoved; the presence of God is changed, and our inner peace is unruffled… it becomes evident that the breaking of the outward man is the basis for enjoying God's presence…."

As stated, I perceive this as a will modification process. Scriptures make clear that Moses' will was broken before he was used. Paul had a light come from heaven and knock him to the ground. A voice came from heaven and said, "Saul, Saul, why persecutest thou me?" When Paul became convinced that this was God speaking directly to him, he changed dramatically. Peter is my favorite. He vowed during the events of Calvary that he would remain faithful. Jesus predicted that he would deny Him three times. Peter not only denied him, but he then went off and wept. Let's remember that it was Peter who led the first church in Jerusalem. This "will modification" process was part of his preparation.

I know that to some this process can be devastating, and sometimes God's purposes are difficult to understand. But He wants our will. I think of Joni Erikson Tadas. She was paralyzed as a teenager, and she has spent her life in a wheelchair, but God had a special touch and a special ministry for her. Many years ago, I had the privilege of interviewing her on radio. As we were discussing the victories and traumas of her life, I asked what might seem to be a ridiculous question. I said, "Joni, do you consider yourself handicapped?" I will never forget her answer. She replied, "Not anymore." It is safe to assume that she had moved through this principle. The breaking of the outer person had opened the inner person.

The principle to be learned is simple. Have we understood the purposes behind our crises?

Change Number Four: The Inner Man has been released. God desires to heal us. Hebrews 12:12-13, "Wherefore lift up the hands which hang down, and the feeble knees; and make straight paths for your feet, lest that which is lame be turned out of the way, but let it rather be healed." And note that after the healing we are admonished to "follow peace with all men." (14) Can we imagine a world where all human spirits "universally" are healed? Can we imagine a world where the first response of our spirit and soul are not to hate, or to be angry, or to kill, but our first response is to make peace? Let's start striving for a healing of our spirit, and hope that this truth can become universal. So many of us are carrying wounds from the past. Tragically, for some, Satan has gotten a "foothold" in our lives, and through his distortion and perversion the healing process has become more difficult. Let's stop for a minute and ask the Lord for a healing. Please pray with me.

"Dear Father, I am so tired of carrying the baggage from my life. I know that I have been in bondage, but dear Father I want to be released. Forgive me for violating your principles and living within my own flesh. I want to pray specifically for my sin of an argumentative spirit and also for (any others)_____. Dear Father, in Jesus' name I acknowledge the working of the Holy Spirit within me and I acknowledge your desire to change me. I

know you want to free me. I ask for a healing now,
and I thank you for it. In Jesus' name."

According to Watchmen Nee, few Christians ever
experience the "release of the spirit." Nee challenges, "There is
an immutable law of God's working in us; His specific purpose
is breaking us and releasing our spirit for free exercise…
whatever the things to which you are bound, God will deal
with them one after another. Not even such trivialities as
clothing, eating, or drinking will escape the careful hand
of the Holy Spirit… until the day comes when <u>all</u> these are
destroyed, you will not know perfect liberty…."

I suppose every church has at least one Aunt Bertha. What
makes Aunt Bertha so special is that she is not preoccupied
with herself. You observe her, as she is, busy loving people.
She cooks for the suppers. She always prays compassionately
for others. It is not unusual for her to be a "hugger." And
somehow her love for people has blinded her to others' faults.
Some within the church might say that she is naive. Let's be
"thankful" that we don't have a whole church of Aunt Berthas.
Can you imagine? Can you imagine a whole block full of Aunt
Berthas, or a city, or a country, or a world? It has to start with
people like you and me.

Ezekiel 18:31 exhorts us to "rid yourselves of all offenses
you have committed, and get a new heart and a <u>new spirit</u>."
Second Corinthians 7:1 states, "Having therefore these
promises, dearly beloved, let us cleanse ourselves from all
filthiness of the flesh and spirit, perfecting holiness in the
fear of God." Ephesians 4:30-32 states that we should, "grieve

not the Holy Spirit of God, whereby ye are sealed unto the day of redemption. Let all bitterness, and wrath, and anger, and clamor and evil speaking, be put away from you, with all malice. And be ye kind one to another, tenderhearted, forgiving one another, even as God for Christ's sake hath forgiven you."

Watchmen Nee cautions us that the "release of the spirit" cannot happen "artificially." I believe his thought is that ultimately God must do it for us. James 4:8 admonishes us that if we "draw nigh to God… He will draw nigh to [us]." This is so true. The healing of the spirit cannot happen by taking pills or doing exercises, or we would all do it. It does start however, I contend, with a "contrite spirit" and with a "hunger and thirst after righteousness." And we do have the promise that if we have that hunger, God will fill us (Matt. 5:6). I hope that the realization has led to a rebuilding. Now we all have the most difficult stage, that of reinforcement. May God's grace and mercy surround us as we practice perfection. Indeed may there be a healing of your argumentative spirit.

THE EPILOGUE

Thank you for taking this journey with me. This has been both an academic and spiritual trip. I certainly need to thank my wife and family for their tolerance and forgiveness. But it is interesting that through the stresses of marriage, life, and raising children, I was forced, I contend, by God to gain insights. The Scriptures relate that "in everything" we should give thanks. I am thankful for a rough childhood, I am thankful for a strong-willed father, and I am thankful for the three times that I came close to death, especially the car accidents, and I am thankful for all of my stresses. Psalm 139:12-16 relates, "my days were numbered" when I was in my mother's womb. Such an awesome God. Ephesians 1:11 states that "all things happen after the counsel of his will." I contend that the most profound thought that we can think is how the Lord sees before us. God numbered your days also. Perhaps from God's perspective, I took my journey, in part, for you. "May the Lord bless you and keep you. May the Lord make His face to shine upon you, and give you peace."